The North Door

Echoes of Slavery in a New England Family

✳

GRANT HAYTER-MENZIES

foreword by Lora-Ellen McKinney

afterword by Daryl D'Angelo

Grant Hayter-Menzies

Cataloguing information

Hayter-Menzies, Grant; D'Angelo, Daryl
The North Door: Echoes of Slavery in a New England Family / Grant Hayter-Menzies, Daryl D'Angels
Includes illustrations

ISBN-978-0-9978941-7-2 (paperback)

Cover art: Suzanne Korn landscape and 1840 sampler edging courtesy of Philadelphia Museum of Art, Whitman Sampler Collection, gift of Pet, Incorporated, 1969-288-317.

In remembrance of
Susan Hutchison
and the Rev. Dr. Samuel Berry McKinney

To Rudi and Freddie
with love

The author is donating all of his royalties from sales of this book to The Slave Dwelling Project and Coming to the Table.

One need not be a Chamber—to be Haunted—

- Emily Dickinson

Se wo were fi na wosankofa a yenkyi

It is never wrong to go back
for that which you have forgotten.

- African proverb

ACKNOWLEDGMENTS

On Christmas Eve 2015, my brother Sean and I did something which some forty odd years earlier we could never have imagined. We stood in a snowy field behind our grandparents' old house in Mariposa, California, flakes absorbing all sounds—even those of our breathing—as we remembered a man buried back there in a featureless grave.

How often as children had we crept upstairs to sleep in that house, in a room the windows of which gave out toward that field, and thought with fear of that grave.

In it, our grandfather assured us, lay the bones of an African American man, a former slave, who had come to Mariposa in its nineteenth century gold rush heyday and died there as handyman to the family which had once owned the land on which our grandparents' house stood.

That land had been subdivided and did not belong to our grandparents, but they told us to remember the man, whose name they didn't know and which could not be read on his weathered and mossy headstone, and to be respectful if we were ever in the field.

We were pretty sure we would never want to be out there, and never did see the stone except from a distance.

Years later, the stone was removed and the exact location of the grave forgotten.

But my experiences at Rose Jackson's grave in Old Saybrook and under the flowering tree at Bush-Holley House in Greenwich moved me to want to do something to acknowledge this man's life. So that Christmas Eve, Sean and I took incense and water, crawled through the snarls of a rusted barbed wire fence, and stood where our hearts told us the man's remains lay.

We'd intended to sing a Christmas carol, but Sean said, "Let's listen to the silence. It's been his music for a very long time now."

And so we did, as snow drifted down in the quiet darkness. Though we said nothing, there was a hymn in the chill air. And a sense that, for perhaps the first time in living memory, a man who was truly one of history's forgotten ones had been remembered on this holy evening celebrating the birth of the supremely good man who told his followers to love no matter what.

And that love, even when sent into the darkness of a snowy field, as into the impenetrable fabric of time, is never wasted.

I owe much to my parents for bringing us up in a home where all humankind was seen as equal, regardless of color or gender or any other "difference" manufactured to leverage privilege and power. My mother was particularly influential in this. For her, the fight for civil rights was a personal one. As a girl in her 1950s Central California high school, where segregation was unknown, she had had many girlfriends of color. I heard that on at least one occasion, Mom, who was attractive, funny and popular, had been "fought" over by two groups of these African American girlfriends. A friend told me of seeing my mother standing in the middle, laughing, as girls on one side and girls on the other, also laughing, tried to claim her physically as one of their own, an honorary sister. My mother was proud of that honor. For her, African American culture stood for glamour, pizzazz, and the inexplicable joy she took in what can only be described by the French phrase "*vive la différence*"— the celebration of what made black culture unique, which a white person like my mother admired all the more for blooming, and blooming fiercely, in such rocky soil. To her, that uniqueness was ammunition in the battle for freedom, one which moved her, the quintessence of a free spirit, all her life, just as seeing it quashed brought her to anger. My mother died nine months after I spent the night in the Bush-Holley House slave quarters. When I called her to tell her about meeting Guy Drock's descendants, and about Rose Jackson, and the libation under the tree, she was quiet, and I knew she was in tears. But her voice was strong. "Thank you," she said. "Thank you for finding them. Thank you for remembering them"—as Nina wished us to remember.

If not for others whom I must thank and remember, this book could never have been written.

The first of my African American cousins to reach out to me was Melenda Gatson Hunter. Melenda and I share DNA, and I also matched her father, as did my brother, who had taken the test to help refine our results. Melenda and I believed we knew where our connection came in—the Lambright family in Mississippi. The evidence, if such it could be called, was wildly circumstantial. Not so circumstantial, though, was a completely unexpected cousin connection Melenda brought to our relationship. She was related to Daisy Gatson Bates (1914-1999), mentor of the Little Rock Nine who in 1957 integrated Central High School despite verbal and physical threats from the Arkansas governor down to the good citizens of Little Rock. Through a descendant of people my white ancestors had victimized because of their race, I ironically had a family connection to African American civil rights royalty.

My cousin Dr. Joanne Walker Flowers was the first of my African American cousins to visit me in Canada. As I have told her so often, she is in many physical respects my mother reborn. An epidemiologist, ordained minister, officer of the U.S. Navy, former chaplain in a prison hospice, and an inveterate genealogist, Joanne is also all the things my mother admired, and she has my mother's sense of humor, which was as much challenge as wit. She also has my mother's sense of history. That first day, Joanne asked if we could sit down and together look at the copies of slave inventories. This was the first time I would do so with an African American person connected to me through slavery. I began to read how my ancestors' human property was disposed of. As Joanne listened intently, I spoke the names of James Wise's slaves. Judy. Sarah. March. Ginette. Satin. Oliver. Buell. Warren. Moses. Then I had to stop, because I couldn't say anything more. "Cousin, you need to get some perspective!" Joanne said. "You act as if *you* held these people as slaves. You didn't. Somewhere back in time, someone in your family held one of my ancestors in slavery, and fathered a child with her, and here we are." "I wish it had not happened," I said. "But it did," Joanne told me. "I wish slavery had never happened, either, but it did, not to mention the ongoing racism and bigotry in America to this very day. As upsetting as all of this is, I have hope because some way, somehow, we survived. And this fact forms the foundation of my faith. But, let us not forget, in meeting and getting to know each other, a healing process has begun and we are closing a circle broken so many years ago and becoming family. And I like you, cousin." I told her I wished that what joined us was not this origin based in pain. Joanne shrugged. "But, here we are," she said. "And what we're doing will change tomorrow. And that's all we can ever be responsible for." Thank you, Joanne, for your kind heart and your courageous belief in truth. What we're doing today will change tomorrow.

I am grateful for the guidance and wisdom of other kind friends and relations over the course of this journey of three centuries: Amy Adams; Dr. Sandra L. Ballard; Toni Renée Battle; Crosby Beene, Jr.; Bernice Bennett; Daryl D'Angelo; Dr. Pamela Kyle Crossley; Thomas Norman DeWolf; Dr. Allegra di Bonaventura; Torrance Downes; Vicci Flatt; Dr. Patricia Penn Hilden; Melenda Gatson Hunter; Rev. J. Hugh A. James; Janice Kincaid; Suzanne Korn; Dionne Ford Kurtti; Joseph McGill; Dr. Lora-Ellen McKinney; Rev. Dr. Samuel Berry McKinney; Rhoda McKinney-Jones; Dr. Debra Mecky; Sharon Leslie Morgan; Rev. David Pettee; Dale Plummer; Donald Roddy; Linda Durr Rudd; Gracelaw Simmons; Kate Starr; Wil Starr; Michael Twitty; Jaime Villaneda; Dr. John Wilson.

FOREWORD

Lora-Ellen McKinney

The North Door: Echoes of Slavery in a New England Family is about slavery practiced outside of the U.S. South, personal family complicity in the economic machine that traded in, used and brutalized human beings for their unpaid labor, and commitment to accountability to those related to the author by blood whom his forebears had physically, spiritually and psychically harmed. *The North Door's* topic is not easy, nor unfortunately, is it uncommon but it is beautifully written, exceptionally rendered and humbly offered. And it is about my family.

As a child, I often asked adults to regale me with tales about the most interesting places they had ventured in the shoes they were wearing. While it was unconventional question for a kindergartner to ask, it was a more important query than they or I could then have known; my question foretold my wish to deeply understand the paths people took, whether familial, pedestrian or exotic, the places they landed, and their interpretation of the experiences that awaited them.

I was as interested in other people's stories as I was my own. As I imagined travel to far-flung locales, I pondered whether understanding my ancestry would enlighten or change my assessment of my future. An African American woman born with bright red hair and a smattering of Irish freckles, I was sufficiently pale that I was swapped with an olive-toned Italian infant. Reclaiming me as theirs, my brown-skinned parents reminded confused hospital staff of Mendel's Law and variability in the skin colors and hair textures expressed in African American genes.

The increased availability of ancestry-driven DNA testing afforded me access to the places my genealogical shoes had traveled. While family stories and my incessant questions painted for me a widening portrait of my background, there remained many unknowns that I anticipated ancestral DNA would better uncover. My pale skin - now browner - freckles and curly hair told me with no tests required, that in me, at a minimum, were the cells and stories of the enslaved and the enslaver. Some of my black elders were so traumatized by past memories that they either doled their lives out to me in palatable chunks or not at all. DNA exploration, I hoped, would make clearer the part of my history that is a primary source of America's shame.

August 2019 marks the 400th anniversary of the arrival of the first documented African slaves to the shores of Old Point Comfort in the English colony of Virginia, where began the "trend in colonial America where people of Africa were taken unwillingly from their homeland, transplanted, and committed to lifelong slavery and racial discrimination."[1]

American slavery is considered a sin of the South. In addition to their assumed higher moral fiber, the Union had twice the number of states, people, and railroad tracks as the southern Confederacy, in addition to a more diverse economic base than a Confederacy built on King Cotton. Resources, more than scruples, won the war.

Based on generations of tales shared in his family, primary source research and DNA findings, Grant Hayter-Menzies has produced an exceptional work about the role and impact of slavery in his family. Beautifully written, with an honesty, vulnerability and bravery typically avoided by white men, *The*

[1] H.R. 4539, Congressional Bill to establish the 400 Years of African American History Commission Act, submitted by Ms., Committee on Energy and Natural Resources, September 6, 2019.

North Door: Echoes of Slavery in a New England Family, exposes a lesser known fact of our history, that the peculiar institution of slavery also fueled the economic engine of the North.

Grant's story, shared with him in tales and artifacts by his maternal grandmother, Nina Stawser, details the complicated history of a Connecticut family that benefited from the trade, holding and oversight of enslaved Africans. Nina proffers this important warning:

> "All of us who benefit from the institution of slavery yet do not acknowledge it, whether we are Southern or Northern, descended from slave-owners or recent immigrants to this nation, are part of the problem— the problem not just of forgetting, but of remembering without learning."

This Connecticut interface may be where the strands of Grant's and my DNA converge. We are third or fourth cousins, related through his mother and my father. Having submitted DNA to five commercial ancestry companies, I increased my potential understanding my genealogic past. Of my newly discovered white family, Grant was the most receptive to my invitation to jointly discover our shared history.

Finding Your Roots is an award-winning PBS show, developed and hosted by Dr. Henry Louis Gates. The esteemed scholar, states the show's website, has "unearthed the family histories of influential people helping shape our national identity." On a recent weekend, I watched several episodes of the show less interested in celebrity than in unearthing secrets more fascinating than the celebrities through whom each story flowed. Consistent across several genealogical histories that I viewed that Saturday were two factors: 1) most of those profiled were deeply moved to learn about their forebears, though most seemed never to have deeply considered who cobbled their genetic paths and 2) many profiles revealed multiple generations of unknown relatives whose strengths and struggles were strongly expressed in the lives of the profiled generation.

Family history is cellular. Genetic genealogy is now routinely used to excavate and identify the genetic relationship between specific individuals. An Ancestry.com commercial announces that "when Courtney McKinney discovered her motherland, she found where her strength was born."[2] Grant and I know the bones of our strength, that the fight for racial justice is our familial birthright. It is in my father's and his mother's Civil Rights activism, my work for equity in pediatric health, Nina's insistence on sharing painful family history and in Grant's dogged commitment to obeying his mother's last wish that he make amends to his black relatives, the descendants of Africans enslaved by his Northern white family. As asked in one of the most beautiful songs in *Hamilton: An American Musical*, "who lives, who dies, who tells your story?"

The gifts of and limitations inherent in genetic genealogy are overlaid by our country's inability to manage the stains of slavery. Maslow's hierarchy of needs does not accommodate the ways that individuals are shaped by shared history. Though borne of a fraught past, the present tense of our DNA stories insists on our specific familial and generally human connections. Our most adaptive choice is to accept our stories as part of us, our history as contextual and to breathe forgiveness into yesteryear for the worst of what we know.

Following a long trip across the waterways that connected our two countries, Grant welcomed me and my puppy Scout

---

[2] Courtney McKinney Ancestry.com ad: When Courtney discovered her motherland,she found where her strength was born   https://www.ancestry.com/cs/courtney.

for a holiday visit. Though we had emailed and talked for several years, within minutes of our meeting Nina emerged in my gestures. We were astonished to discover that Grant, his brother, Sean, and I have the same rare quirk of neurology that bathes our brains in music.

To formally celebrate Boxing Day 2014, Grant and I ate an impossibly delicious meal of poppy seed-laden, gluten-free bread and jam, a salad of bitter greens, mushroom loaf with vegetable gravy, almonds, pear slices, dried apricots and piping hot green tea. Sitting across from one another at a small table in a home where every object - family heirlooms, gifts from friends and personally selected acquisitions – breathed history, my cousin and I smiled at one another and invited every conflicted ancestor to the table.

After supper, we walked my irrepressible Scout and his somewhat reticent Freddie around his small seaside town, the skies resplendent with the gloss of a bone-chilling winter sun. Standing at the majestic junction of British Columbia's Gulf Islands and the US San Juan Islands, we marveled at the inner identifiable sameness that resided within our opposing social labels. We casually perambulating cousins, one tree-toppingly tall black female American woman and one white dual citizen of Canada and the United States who proudly owned his path to pride as a gay man, imagined ourselves as we actually were: one singular sensation, the only creatures like us in the entire town.

Stories are our most important tradition, an essential tool for familial and cultural preservation. Individually, they translate our familial and cultural remembering into myth. Myth becomes the bridge over which we recognize one another. What then is left? A determination to engage a new standard of behavior. To embrace and talk through our pasts and our possibilities. What is left, hopefully, is the willingness to accept the shame in our family trees. Increasingly rare in these fraught times, connection through story is our gift to the future of our family and the family of man.

In 2015, the McKinneys and Menzies first found that willingness sitting in the McKinney family room in Seattle. A nervous Grant reached gently to an aging man, new to him but deeply and recognizably his kin, and read to him the narrative of this book about the pained traces of family, outlining the gnarls on our particular tree. Our pasts, present and future - individual and shared – later aligned a car on a Seattle corner on warm and windy Mother's Day in 2015. My father insisted on a parking space next to the First Presbyterian Church that a half-century earlier had rescinded their invitation for my father's friend, Martin Luther King, Jr. to speak to a Seattle audience. In 1998, having learned of this blemish on their Christian witness, the congregation's new pastor asked my father for forgiveness. It was given. In obedience to his mother's deathbed wish, Grant then asked his elder cousin for forgiveness. A Civil Rights icon held his newly discovered cousin's hand and blessed him with a gift, a gently prayerful recommendation that we can only move forward. Forgiveness granted and accepted for the sins of Grant's fathers and mothers, we cousins relaxed into the best of what is gained from these DNA journeys. We faced one another, unpacked our stories and leaned into love.

CONTENTS

1 INTRODUCTION

It's a setting which anyone who has gone camping will recognize. Lying in darkness on padding that fails to keep your spine and shoulder blades from uncomfortable contact with an unyielding surface just below your sleeping bag. Darkness that seems to engulf you once the small light source is doused. Pattering of rain on a thin membrane a couple of feet over your face. Silence so deep your own thoughts echo.

Below me were elegant rooms hung with priceless artworks and peopled by antique chairs and tables, highboys and sideboards and four poster beds. The walls were stylishly papered, the windows draped in lovely fabrics, the floors in Persian rugs.

My sleeping space, by contrast, was the epitome of sparse: bare boards, small, uncurtained dormer windows, beams too low to avoid striking your head on them in darkness. And it was cold, though easy to imagine the opposite at height of summer.

On March 30-31, 2012, I experienced all of those things, but not in a tent at a campsite. I lay on the floorboards of an attic over a kitchen in a sprawling eighteenth century house located just off the I-95 in Cos Cob, a suburb of Greenwich, Connecticut.

I spent that night in the former slave quarters of Bush-Holley House. With me were three other people. One of them was Joseph McGill, a descendant of enslaved African Americans. He founded the Slave Dwelling Project, an organization which aims to help draw attention to and preserve extant former dwellings of enslaved people in America by spending the night in them.

The other two overnighters were Dionne Ford Kurtti and the Rev. David Pettee. Dionne descends from enslaved and enslavers in Louisiana. Dave, with whom I share Connecticut ancestry and white skin, descends from dozens of New England ancestors who held slaves throughout the region.

Together, in memory of a history that few of us were taught anything about at school, we slept under the Bush-Holley House eaves, in living quarters which had offered the Bush family's slaves a brief sliver of privacy and autonomy between night's duties done downstairs and dawn's shining on duties awaiting them there.

What still strikes me is how surreal this experience was. We were in slave quarters, but we were not in Natchez, Mississippi, or Charleston, South Carolina or Mobile, Alabama. We were in Greenwich, Connecticut, about as Yankee a bastion of Abolition and the Underground Railroad as one could find. And the people who had slept in this attic had been legally enslaved until as late as 1848, eleven years before the Civil War broke out and, with it, the impending end of slavery.

My journey back to that New England attic began thirty-five years ago when I, a teenager, first delved into the ancestry of my grandmother, a woman born in the South.

I come from a remembering family, and my maternal grandmother, Nina Lewis Strawser (1913-2001), was the memory keeper in chief.

Nina remembered because, as a child, she was not afraid to ask questions of old people, and they trusted her enough to vouchsafe to her hazy but compelling recollections about slaves in the family. For my grandmother, the past, along with its glories and its sins, was very much alive. It was a characteristic I would come to see as a basic component of Southern heritage, where if what is past for most people is past because it is finished, what is past for the Southerner is still present because an identity, a "cause", a mythical but no less revered "way of life", was wounded but not killed by the Civil War, even for those who see no romance in Old Dixie. It lives on in the relatively harmless potboiler material of novels and costume dramas, and also in the boundlessly harmful resentment that fuels a host of hatreds, bitterest among them racism. Nina remembered because remembering was tied inextricably to compassion—the responsibility for saving what she cared about from being forgotten.

The word *sankofa*, from the Twi language of Ghana, translates to "go back and get it", as in the phrase "*Se wo were fi na wosankofa a yenkyi*", "It is not wrong to go back for that which you have forgotten," and is often rendered in symbolic form by a bird whose body faces forward while its head, with an egg in its beak, looks back. *Sankofa* seems to best describe Nina's kind of remembering. It moved my grandmother to fill scrapbooks with vignettes of photographs, pressed flowers, a silk baby stocking, stanzas of poetry clipped from magazines, her father's love letters to her mother. Remembering also compelled her to preserve the referred pain of that other Southern wound, never healed, as if putting away what was broken for a day when she could make an attempt to mend it: Slavery, and her family's role in exploiting it, supporting it, and then forgetting it. Except for Nina, who couldn't forget.

I thought of *sankofa* when I read Edward Ball's *Slaves in the Family*, Ball's account of delving into his Southern family's past of vast South Carolina rice plantations and just as vast ownership of slaves, and his efforts to trace the latter's descendants, many of them his cousins—my family history but on a far greater scale. He opens the book with a conversation about what to a Southern family is one of the most contentious, emotional, and oft avoided topics. According to Ball's father, the five topics never aired in the family were religion, sex, death, money, and the Negroes. Ball's mother asked what that left to talk about. His father said, jokingly, "That's another of the family secrets."[1]

The fifth topic forbidden at the Ball dinner table was similarly not discussed in Nina's immediate family, for two significant reasons. Because slavery's presence in our domestic history was hinted at but not confirmed, it seemed to belong more to myth than reality. And because, like many terrible truths shelved to be the more easily forgotten, slavery in our family history was easier to keep at a distance the farther we moved from it in chronological terms. No one in our family ever ventured to sound its depths.

It would be an exaggeration to claim that Nina did. She could care as much about her link to slavery as she did and yet still operate within the matrix of paternalistic southern beliefs. "I seem to be sitting astraddle of the fence of time," she wrote in an unpublished essay from 1970, "and looking on both sides of it at once, seeing things in retrospect as well as prospect." Her link to slavery worried her, but so did other more contemporary issues—the endless, useless war in Vietnam, the fraught politics of the Sixties and Seventies, the race riots. She admired Cesar Chavez, the California activist, supported his cause and went to witness his final hunger strike. Beyond that, she did what a lady of her time and place did. She crocheted useful items to send to poor children in Africa. She went to church every Sunday, praying in her white gloves for the souls of all who suffered. But she never tried to sidestep her own deeply curious, deeply compassionate nature, even when that meant, while visiting the

---

[1] Ball, *Slaves in the Family*, 7.

rambling old house of our family history, she opened doors to find unnerving surprises waiting for her.

For Nina, satisfying curiosity about the past was not just a polite gesture, or a cue for pleasant chitchat. It was a duty to remember and to pass memory on to those most grateful to receive and most apt to protect it. Above all, having reached into the memories of elderly relatives, many old enough to have been brought up in households where black people were personal property, Nina had also grown up in a South in the grip of white backlash against blacks after the Civil War and a botched Reconstruction failed to reorder those racial dynamics which, for as long as anyone could remember, had put white over black in a hierarchy many Southerners believed ordained by God.

That was not a God my devout grandmother recognized. Nina, who had moved to California in the early 1930s, once told me she frankly hated the South. I think it was not the remembering that drove her away from the culture of her birth and that of her ancestors back to the seventeenth century. With the duty to remember was the duty to reclaim, and with that reclamation the promise of *sankofa*, to go back for the thing you forgot and learn from that forgetting how to do better. What Nina experienced in the South was a denial of what she saw as self-evident truth, that all human beings, white and black, are made in the image of God.

This woman who, on a visit to Washington D.C. in 1977, had sat for an hour in the Lincoln Memorial, meditating on words engraved in marble—"a new nation conceived in liberty and dedicated to the proposition that all men are created equal"… "to do all which may achieve and cherish a just and lasting peace among ourselves and with all nations"— saw national unity in perhaps the same way Lincoln did, as a brotherhood ordained by their Creator, regardless of race or creed, bound by common blood. The reality of the South, where those ideals were not put into practice, was one she ultimately had to flee, unable to witness its crimes any further. Like the *sankofa* bird, she didn't, couldn't, turn away from that past, even as she knew she had to press on toward the future. Yet it was not lost on Nina that that nightmare was one that she, a white woman, was as free to escape as its principal victims, Southern blacks, were not.

Along with a post-Civil War bowed-top Saratoga trunk, a baby dress mended by the black woman who was, for Nina, a nexus of love and regret, and hundreds of letters written in her firm but graceful hand, I inherited remembering from my grandmother, and it is her remembering that sent me on the journey this book describes. Nina didn't know which of her ancestors were enslavers, and she didn't know anything about any of people who were enslaved. She remembered plenty of tales told her by her grandmother, who bore the Southern Gothic name of Amaryntha Culpepper, about Yankees coming and valuables hurriedly hidden. There was an account of how a female cousin somewhere in the Deep South had met Union troops on her front porch and sassed them when they asked her for provisions. This lady emerged unharmed, but not so Nina's great-grandfather, who was lassoed and dragged by the leg down a road for picking up his gun in the presence of Union soldiers. Amid these detailed recollections, there were no remembered nicknames of black nurses or cooks, drivers or field hands.

Only fifty-five years had elapsed between Nina's birth in 1913 and the 1858 death of James Wise, last of our family's slave owners, whose enslaved people were auctioned in 1864, during the death throes of the Confederacy. Did nobody record or remember Moses who, after the war, came to live with his wife and children next door to his former owner's son in Claiborne Parish, Louisiana? How had Judy, senior female among the Wise slaves and doubtless nurse to more than one generation of the family, simply vanished from memory? Nina's grandmother easily recalled girlhood memories of playing under the big trees on her grandparents' plantation, or learning poetry from her family's live-in tutor, a young man who later died at Gettysburg, or hiding things from approaching Union soldiers. But what about the names of the black people who had faithfully served her family? They became invisible, consigned to the anonymous and dispassionate hands of census takers, whose records were to inform me of their statistical existence a century and a half later.

When I did show Nina the inventories of the human beings our ancestors owned and worked in house and field, she was silent. But her compassion did not flinch. She had guessed as much; the documentation was merely supporting evidence. Her photographic memory of afternoons spent with her elders, and of growing up in a South where black people were still seen as 3/5 of a person, had offered her too many plausible hints to question veracity when proofs came. "I have always wondered who they were," Nina told me, referring to her ancestors' slaves. "I have always wondered what happened to them after the war—where they went, what they did. If they were happy."

This is why, seeing her hands gently touching those lists of names and prices, I began research to see if I could find them for her. At least at first, that is, that was the plan. By the time Nina died, I sought to find them for me. Finally, I realized I had to find them, and remember them, for themselves.

Mine is not a particularly unique journey. From Ball's *Slaves in the Family* to Michael Twitty's *The Cooking Gene*, memoirs, biographies and histories of slavery in America, and of the black and white dynamic of the peculiar institution, with concomitant journeys across landscapes earthly and of soul, have enriched our knowledge, raised troubling questions, staked new cultural territory and kindled controversies that in truth have never stopped burning. And the American public at large, who may never have read Ball or Twitty or even Alex Haley, has still been sensitized to the roles of individuals and the arc of ideologies in history by an ever burgeoning fascination with genealogy. We live in an era where, for at least the past forty years, genealogical research has gone from presumed passing fad of the eccentric to a normalized activity to be found in virtually every family, with hundreds of how-to books, memoirs, television shows, DNA testing companies to meet increasing demand. Many family researchers are sorting fact from fiction in their personal histories and, in so doing, sorting them out in the broader history of the United States, where fact and fiction have never really been at peace. This goes for the claim that antebellum slavery was relatively uncommon, a claim meant to absolve the South of the indictment that helped lead it into war. A meme circulated during the first year of Donald J. Trump's presidency, signed by a "Proud Southern Deplorable", claimed that "at the peak of slavery in 1860, only 1.4% of Americans owned slaves," in an apparent effort to justify the South's position in the Civil War as being on states' rights ground alone. However, as Washington College historian Adam Goodheart, author of *1861: The Civil War Awakening* (Knopf, 2011) points out, 1860 Census data shows that over 25% of Southern households owned slaves. In Mississippi, for example, close to half of households were slave-owning.

From this it is reasonable to infer that many more white people living today, particularly in the South but—as I was to find—also in the North, are likely to descend from enslavers than most know. So my descent from enslavers, through Nina's Deep South ancestry, is not special. But as I've said, we are a remembering family, and that is not as common. Thanks to careful preservation of memory, for me names in old family Bibles and in official government records have faces, even characteristic gestures and voices, going back before the Civil War, and each plays a definitive role in shaping what I think of them and their times and in shaping my own beliefs against the backdrop of their lives.

This is why Nina, though born almost fifty years after the end of the Civil War, and meeting but a handful of elders predating that cataclysm, felt as strongly about slavery as if she had lived in its midst, not least because throughout her childhood and youth in east Texas, she had also witnessed racism firsthand. She had seen the way her father, a cotton farmer with ideas of racial equality ahead of his time, and her mother, descendant of Deep South planters with more conservative views on the subject, interacted with Mrs. Daniel, the black woman who did the family's laundry, whom Nina knew and loved as Aunt Sammy. She had seen the violent influence of organized racism, in form of the Ku Klux Klan, on blacks and whites in her Texas community, had had frightening experience of its warning shots directed at white people who dared to become "familiar" with black people.

Whereas in my research into my Southern ancestry I found much to give me pause, I believed by turning to my Northern ancestors I would find much to comfort me—perhaps, too, much to let me off the hook, to feel superior to those cotton fields and slave cabins.

One of Nina's Tennessee-born ancestors had had a mother born in colonial Connecticut where, so far as I was concerned, I was safe from the South. New England was little more complicated than that to me, at least then. I had been taught the received catechism. The South had started the Civil War over its support for a slavery that the North condemned. The North had defeated the South to end slavery; a strictly Southern institution and a crime against humanity was thus eradicated from the face of God's green earth.

Thus New England had been the sacred instrument for breaking the shackles of the enslaved.

And yet it was there I would uncover evidence that my Southern heritage of African American enslavement did not stop somewhere in the early nineteenth century at the northernmost reaches of the Mason-Dixon Line. I would find that my family in seventeenth and eighteenth century New England—in Massachusetts, Connecticut, Rhode Island—had also owned slaves, and that taking Africans captive and exploiting them had a history in my bloodline that stretched back to 1555, to the very eve of the traditional beginnings of the transatlantic slave trade courtesy of slaving pioneer John Hawkins in 1562. In those pleasant two-dimensional sampler farmhouses with their cross-stitch blue skies, enslaved African and Native American people lived, worked, were born and died, living and working alongside my ancestors but buried apart from them, what privacy they had briefly enjoyed in attics or cellars or hallways outside the kitchen chamber. And like my post-Civil War Southern forebears and the people they had enslaved, we as a nation collectively forgot the people enslaved by our colonial New England antecedents.

Where it had proved impossible to locate descendants of people purchased and worked by my Southern ancestors, in the heart of New England, of all places, I was to meet by sheer accident the progeny of Guy Drock, a Cameroonian man enslaved by my forebears in Norwich, Connecticut, then sold away from them under unique circumstances. Our reunion proved complex, moving, frustrating not just to me but to Drock's descendants, who were at first and for some time to come unsure, if not suspicious, of my motives in wishing to connect with them. I, too, had my uncertainties, which redoubled when I helped organize the sleepover at Bush-Holley House described at beginning of this narrative, confronting questions not in Nina's remembered voice but in the stronger one of my own twenty-first century con-science: Why are you doing this? Who are you doing it for? Is it enough that Nina cared, that you care? Is the fact you care of any use to those you care about? Was I merely lever-aging my white privilege in a paternalistic feel-good exercise benefiting my own ego?

Another level of my research, that of having my DNA test-ed with 23andMe, brought an unexpected invitation from African American cousins, my relatives through Nina, who lived in Seattle, again far from the South, but with whom I share blood, bone and history. My elderly cousin, the Rev. Dr. Samuel Berry McKinney, a social justice warrior famed in the Pacific Northwest for bringing family friend and schoolmate Dr. Martin Luther King, Jr. to Seattle, listened to my apology for a past over which I had no control but for which I felt Nina's need to atone, then read me a lesson in remembering what really matters—that while present tears for past sins are commendable to a point, the sins in ques-tion are not mine. Mine, however, is the opportunity to help make changes in the now to help heal the wounds from then. They are wounds still fresh and never allowed to heal because America's original sin is not so much slavery, per se, but the racism which gave it permission to exist. America's ongoing responsibility is to do everything needed to solve the problems racism causes and is caused by in an eternal vicious circle, even when nobody, from the commander in chief on down, cares very much about it. And faced with that responsibility, many would see *sankofa* as far too ardu-ous—that even the cosmic mistake of chattel slavery is too tough an error to go back and fix, to remember and not for-get.

I found that the end of my journey was just its beginning. Setting myself free, ultimately, was beside the point. Honor-ing and remembering the lives of the enslaved—going back and acknowledging them and their sacrifices—was the point, as Nina always knew.

Like any road trip, my journey included stretches of feature-less terrain interrupted by high hills difficult to climb, with deep valleys and all the good and bad that come with travel, particularly into regions of which the traveler knows very little.

But this journey was also the act of gaining entry to and then investigating each chamber of a very old house.

It's a house haunted by the ghosts of ancestors past, a dwelling with Tudor foundations, Stuart staircases, Georgian casements, and an attic crowded with the rich detritus of generations of wealth derived from exploitation of enslaved human beings. It's a house covered with the tangled vines of interwoven relationships and interdependencies. These vines embrace, even strangle, but they hold the structure together. In every room of that house, I find not only the faces of my white ancestors looking back at me, but the faces, too, of the African and Native American people they enslaved. I don't look away.

In an era in America and, indeed, around the world, where many are turning away from facts of history laid bare to fictions raised by exploitative fantasists peddling the discord (and, for some, the opportunity) of racism, nationalism and xenophobia, facing America's slavery past at first seems a nonissue. Of course it matters, now more than ever. But perhaps it is too easy to nod to the facts of our history, just as it is too easy to deny them, while continuing to ignore how slavery shaped whole nations, economies and blood-lines. The fierce rhetoric and sometimes deadly violence that erupt around Confederate monuments proves, among other things, that we are still very far from a just peace and an un-derstanding of what brought us to this critical juncture—

slavery, its power, its tragedy, and its consequences for future society and politics in America, beyond the land south of the Mason-Dixon Line to New England, birthplace of American abolition, cradle of American slavery.

I hoped to find answers on my journey, both the one I took on planes and trains and the far more arduous one I took trying to write about the experience. I don't know whether I have succeeded or, whether, anyone can. In truth, what matters more than any action is the resolve that precedes it. Before that resolve must come a willingness to face facts—to drink the wine of truth, in Dame Rebecca West's words, "heedless that it is not sweet like milk, but draws the mouth with its strength, and celebrate communion with reality."

2 NINA

My earliest memory is of being carried by Nina (the "i" as in "pie"), my maternal grandmother, when I was less than a year old, to her old white clapboard house that stood just two front yards up the street from ours in my California hometown.

It's a memory of blue: the edge of a blue blanket wrapped around my head, the blue of her eyes smiling down at me, and beyond her face the blue of the sky intercut by leafless branches. The latter belonged to the birches in front of her home. I thought I had dreamed it, but as Nina assured me years later, my memory was based on fact. She had indeed brought me from my parents' house, where my mother lay ill with the mumps and measles (caught from me), to stay with her and Grandpa till my mother recovered.

"You have the gift of memory," Nina once said, recognition and concern in her eyes. "You take after me."

Even as a very young boy, having barely lived myself, I sensed that there was more to what was left untold in the life of a given person. The mystery of how people survived what happened to them fascinated me. In the conversational patter of my elders, I could hear the patterns of past plots and counter-plots, loves lost and won, war and peace and despair. How did they carry on?

Nina's life is only part of the story I am about to tell, but it is the foundation of that larger history, without which the rest cannot stand. And it was in her life that the quest she sent me on, which outlived her and may outlive me, first began. As I have said, we are a remembering family.

Nina was born in Cooke County, Texas on June 27, 1913. Her father was Charles Benjamin Lewis, known as Charlie, a young farmer from Pope County, Arkansas, whose grandfather had been overseer on a plantation in that state and whose grandmother descended from families who had helped found Massachusetts and Connecticut. Nina's mother, Eliza Bartow Kelly, called Lila, was born not far from Waco, Texas, granddaughter to another plantation overseer, her mother connected to a dense web-work of South Carolina, Louisiana and Mississippi slave owners, many of them German in origin, seated on their lands since the end of the eighteenth century.

Nina's credo was as much perpetual curiosity about other people as it was their equal status in the eyes of God. I think it was because of her insistence that everyone had a story as well as dignity that Nina became the repository of so many stories herself. This, and her gifts as a writer, moved her to treat everyone she met as a library to be explored and treasured. And this insistence on the dignity of everyone's lives —especially the lives of those who end up on the margins of society or the footnotes of history—contributed to my becoming a biographer, as it did my later efforts to discover what I could about the people her family had enslaved in the Deep South.

Nina grew up surrounded by history. During her east Texas childhood, she had had two sets of grandparents who lived nearby. She even knew a great-grandmother, Adelia Wise Culpepper, a woman who had grown up waited on by slaves. Her visits to Texas were remembered by Nina for her long black dresses, her habit of taking snuff (considered crude in the early 1920s of Nina's childhood but once fashionable for a rural Mississippi planter's daughter in the 1850s), and her often cutting commentary. I came to meet these people through Nina's memories. Through our talks and her letters, I knew Nina had spent her first few years on a farm belonging to her paternal grandfather, Elijah Clark Lewis, who also owned a store in the nearby village of Mountain Springs, in Cooke County, near where Nina had been born. Some time after 1920, when their middle daughter Vera was born, Charlie and Lila Lewis moved to a farm in Denton County, where the family had as their closest neighbors an African American couple named Henry and Janie (known to Nina as Aunt Sammy) Daniel, who lived on a nearby farm with their daughters.[1]

One of these daughters, Lily Mae, would become my grandmother's dearest childhood friend. Lily Mae's nickname was Scissorbill. The scissorbill or skimmer is a black and white bird seen on the Atlantic coast of the U.S. It's a clever and resourceful bird, its lower bill protruding from under its upper one, giving the effect of a severe under-bite. Out of this collection of traits emerged, at least in my mind, a little girl with a petulant lower lip but bright eyes and quick, decisive movements. Scissorbill seems to have been all of that, and Nina loved her. When Lila was ill, Aunt Sammy was hired to look after the house and Nina, "to do our laundry, using the scrub-board and boiling pot method," Nina said. "She always brought her little girl with her, and the two of us had a great time running and playing."[2]

Shortly after the move to the Denton County farm, Nina's infant sister Vera became very sick. What was wrong with Vera remains a mystery, but her blood pressure had dropped dangerously low. Lacking antibiotics, and often professional doctoring, farm families fell back on home remedies and prayer. My great-grandmother Lila sat with the unconscious child for hours, massaging her wrists to aid circulation, ad-

---

[1] U.S. Census 1920: Year: 1920; Census Place: Pilot Point, Denton, Texas; Roll: T625_1795; Page: 6B; Enumeration District: 56; Image: 937.

[2] Strawser, "A tribute to my era", 2.

ministering whatever remedies seemed called for, and asking God to intervene. Parenting of that day mandated that children be kept out of the way of such serious scenes as the one playing out over the sick baby in the bedroom, though everyone in the family was aware of the possibly tragic outcome. Mrs. Daniel had come to the household's rescue, managing the housework, making sure people were fed. And she had brought Scissorbill with her. She and Nina were told to stay outside and play.

It was while she and Scissorbill were in the yard, Nina said, that she witnessed something that, even as an old lady, she could still conjure in every detail. Through a window, she saw Aunt Sammy in the kitchen ironing Vera's tiny clothes. Nina then heard Sammy talking. Weeping as she ironed, Sammy spoke to each little dress and shirt. "You are going to live, child," Sammy said. "You are going to live!" As she passed the iron over the fabric, and prayed, tears dropped with a hiss on the hot metal.

Mrs. Daniel remained a constant in Nina's heart. It is interesting to me that for the rest of her life, through numerous moves and quick escapes made necessary by my grandfather's rootless and restive mode of living, Nina never lost a little white cotton baby dress, with simple lace insets around the neck and three pearl buttons up the back. The dress had likely been made by Nina's maternal grandmother, Amaryntha Culpepper Kelly, whose fine and detailed work she admired. But she didn't keep it because of that. "Sammy mended it," Nina told me, "when the lace was torn. Pink thread on white lace—you can't miss it." That was all she said, and all she needed to say, about what was, to her, clearly a relic made sacred by the woman who had repaired it. What Nina felt for Aunt Sammy, who had truly been a surrogate mother to her, was not to be doubted by anyone who saw her holding the yellowed dress, its pink thread mending all the more conspicuous, tenderly in her hands. "I loved her," Nina said, simply.

Vera did recover, and had it been Scissorbill who had survived dire illness instead of Vera, Sammy could not have been more overjoyed. As my African-American cousin, psychologist Dr. Lora-Ellen McKinney, put it when she saw the dress that Aunt Sammy mended, "How do we recognize that we have ancestors on opposite sides of the struggles that define human history? How might we best acknowledge those who cared for us? Who loved even when the loving relationship was tainted with inequity?"[3]

This was part of the conundrum of race relations that puzzled, frustrated and saddened my grandmother. Nina recalled the time Mrs. Daniel and her husband came to the Lewis home, not for work but for a visit. The Danielses must have passed through the front yard—perhaps Charlie was talking to Henry about weather, or other farming-related phenomena—and in a sane world it would have seemed natural to anybody to ask them into the house and sit down. This is what Charlie did, conducting Henry and Sammy through the front door and into the living room. His wife Lila could barely contain herself. "Mama was furious," Nina said, "but right in front of them, Daddy told her, 'Be *quiet*.'"

Charlie was a man of principle whose insistence on fairness (he disliked corporal punishment) and love of education were family legend. Knowledge, he believed, set a person free. And where fairness was at question, for Charlie there were certain inalienable rights that needed to be exercised as well as protected. One of these rights was that all men are created equal. Yet for a white man to invite a black man into his house by the front door, as he had done for the Danielses, was simply not something you wanted people to

---

[3] Dr. Lora-Ellen McKinney to author, July 2, 2015.

know about in rural 1920s Denton County or anywhere else throughout the South.

Nina remembered that Charlie had accepted an invitation from some friends and colleagues to an evening meeting. These were men Charlie knew and worked with on a daily basis, with whom he and his family worshipped in church; he was likely related to a few of them, through the myriad of ties that bound a rural community together. What kind of meeting was it? Nina was certain it had to do with the Ku Klux Klan. Founded in Tennessee in 1865, the Ku Klux Klan was constituted as a white vigilante response to perceived federal favoritism shown to freed blacks during Reconstruction. The organization was outlawed not long afterward and its members punished. The Klan and its wizards rose again in the early 1920s, possibly inspired by sympathetic treatment in D. W. Griffith's 1915 film *The Birth of a Nation*, and this time they cleverly threw their weight on the side of Prohibition, as if they were actually just another temperance society.

At that time, the Klan's national office was located in Dallas, about an hour and a half drive south of Gainesville, near where the Lewis family lived, so it is certainly possible a branch of the organization operated locally. Gainesville, which Rand-McNally dubbed "America's Most Patriotic City", a place which boasts a Civil War monument inscribed with the words "no nation rose so white and fair, none fell so pure of crime", has a dark history of clashes between those with different ideas of what patriotism means. It was the brewing pot and the stage for the Great Hanging of October 1862, when dozens of suspected Union sympathizers were lynched, by officials and by mobs. Efforts to tell the truth about this episode have been met with opposition as recently as 2012 from those apparently agreeing that "justice" was served to traitors to the Confederacy. "Gainesville has been hiding from the Great Hanging since it happened," stated one resident with a more nuanced view.[4]

What Charlie thought he was getting into when he attended the "meeting" to which he was invited we may never know. We do know he didn't remain there for long. "Daddy heard the men talking," Nina said. "They were joking about throwing black babies into a fire. And laughing. This made my father sick. He left and never went back."

The Lewises were then living at what Nina called the Cunningham place, a cotton farm located some miles outside Gainesville. Nina believed the property predated the Civil War. She spoke and wrote of this two story farmhouse, with its broad porches and overhanging oak trees, its fireflies bobbing among the flowers in the front yard, as a kind of refuge from the world's disorder.

One winter afternoon, Charlie, as often happened when he was in town on business, was late returning home. Nobody worried. "It was such a peaceful evening," Nina told me, "so ordinary." The Lewis women had had dinner. Nina was sitting with Lila on a broad, deep landing at the top of the steps, lit by flickering kerosene lamps (the house was not wired for electricity). "Mama liked to do her sewing there," Nina told me. The farm itself seemed to have settled into a general repose; the chickens, horses, and other animals were asleep or nearly so; the family's collie, Joe, was dozing beside the kitchen stove. Then all hell broke loose. "Someone fired shots at the house," Nina remembered. The women screamed; Joe barked. It was as if the shooter or shooters were aiming for the windows, of which the lower floor had plenty, covered with nothing more than net curtains. It was buckshot rather than bullets, and they were firing by night,

---

[4] Campbell, "After 150 years, a dark chapter of Gainesville's past still stirs passions," October 7, 2012.

so only one of the windows was damaged, but the front of the house was sprayed with shot. The real damage was inside. Terrified, Lila gathered up Nina and her younger sisters and doused the lights. For what felt like hours, till Charlie came home, mother and daughters crouched and shook on the landing. Clearly, a warning had been given.

When I asked Nina why she had never been back to see the house, she shook her head. Her son had passed through the area in the 1970s and taken some Polaroids of the Gainesville farm which Nina treasured. She had carefully put the photos into an album, which we were perusing as we sat on the sofa together. "I'd rather look at these, honey," she told me. "There were things down there that I don't want to visit again."

In my mid-teens, in what I see now was a naïve effort at best, I introduced myself to my family's history by giving Nina several blank family group sheets, whose empty white blocks for "mother", "grandfather" and "great-grandmother" I asked her to fill in as best she could. I needed to see how much she knew and, where that knowledge was no longer mapped in memory, establish where my exploration into unknown territory must begin. Nina patiently completed the sheets in neat italic capitals, the names and dates often accompanied by footnotes: "I clarified this with Mama" or "Vera remembers it differently."

If I'd always had the colored church window glass of Nina's vivid memories, now we were fashioning the sturdy mullions to hold the pieces in place, gradually forming a picture. And this is where the microscope—and scalpel—of genealogical research entered the scene: the slow, steady plodding through census records, wills, deeds; the overturning of family traditions, and the uncovering of family secrets.

What I found not only corroborated Nina's recollections of stories overheard in her childhood of seven decades earlier, but added a few more pages of history, much of it difficult to process. Of Nina's four great-grandfathers, two were sons of enslaver fathers, two were employed as overseers on plantations in Georgia and Arkansas. Five of her great-great-grandparents descended from enslaver families active in Louisiana, Mississippi, Tennessee, Georgia, North Carolina and South Carolina. Alongside the names of my Culpepper, Wise, Lambright, Anding and Shuler ancestors were the first names, gender and approximate age of other people's ancestors—enslaved adults and children with names like Randall, Isabella, Charity, Moses, Assariah, Satin, Vinia, Wallace, Phebe. (A list of enslaved and enslavers is provided as an addendum to this volume; it is by no means definitive, as new names regularly appear.)

These were not names listed in the script of a Civil War movie or in a novel. They were human beings purchased and worked by my grandmother's—by my—Southern forebears, from the eighteenth century till the middle of the Civil War.

This type of personal discovery, which family researchers sitting in quiet courthouses or libraries in cities and towns across the United States have stumbled over for decades, has been featured countless times on episodes of hit television shows like *Who Do You Think You Are?* or *Finding Your Roots*. On these genealogy gotcha shows, a scripted researcher asks a featured star of film or sports or media to open a manila folder to find a crumbling old will, and to read certain lines conveniently highlighted for the home viewer. The star pauses, or re-reads the passage in question. He or she may sit there, stunned, or smile nervously, or close their eyes, as if that will blot out the facts spread before them.

Decades before these experiences became an expected staple of reality television and a normal part of genealogical research, I had that moment, because in the inventories and wills that arrived in my mailbox and inbox, I now had proof: I had had ancestors who had owned slaves; and I'd had ancestors who supervised—possibly tyrannized—slaves. Later on, thanks to the hard research work of African American cousins who queried me for family records, I would also uncover evidence that I had had ancestors who fathered children with enslaved women.

That first time I showed Nina the slave lists, I remember distinctly how quietly she sat beside me. Her slender hands, usually busy with sewing or housework, rested motionless on the names of human beings that ran, without comma, straight into a list of cattle, horses and sheep, all of these below the ordered columns pricing teapots and sidesaddles and fruit bowls. After a time, my grandmother turned to me, and in a low, quiet voice, she said, in contravention of the legal system of the time but in tandem with her own personal and religious principles, "Had I been alive then, *I would have let them all go.*"

During Nina's lifetime and for years after her death, starting from her initial curiosity, purely abstract in nature, about what had happened to the people her ancestors had enslaved throughout the South, I would try to identify their descendants. I unpack this now, with more maturity and from the other end of the journey, and see the prime motivator— helping Nina as she tried to learn the fate of people who were first purchased by her family, then freed by the United States government to pursue life paths of their own choosing, and whether they had ended up "all right", in her words. I believe this concern was bound up in her compassion for the marginalized in any situation, and that it was likely also prodded by her faith, which made it clear that slavery was a sin and enslavers sinners, and repentance called for by Almighty God. She never said as much, but I knew her heart well. She had to know the truth, however painful it might be.

As a biographer specializing in telling the stories of other people's lives, I needed to know it, too, for all the same reasons and knowing all the same risks.

Good genealogy depends on records, documents, paperwork, and providence watching over courthouses to keep them and their records from going up in flames. Because some did, and the records I sought could not be reconstructed, I was left with nothing, but in other cases, rich sources opened a door into my family's past: an 1864 Louisiana estate sale in which James Wise's slaves purchased items from the plantation where they had labored, only to be sold themselves a month later at auction to pay off the old man's large debts. An intestate estate in North Carolina, in which my deceased ancestor's executors rented out his slaves to family members against their expected inheritance, a dodgy situation his widow took full advantage of by charging room and board for an enslaved woman and her children whom she retained in her household to serve her. Dubious riches, these, because they gave me added insight into a system I already assumed to have been vicious, but saw was even worse than I or Nina could have imagined.

In truth, however, it was in pushing on in my original task—Nina's belief that there were descendants of her ancestors' enslaved people, and that we should try to find out what happened to them—that I experienced the keenest challenge. This was the proverbial "brick wall", genealogists' shorthand for an insurmountable paucity of documentation linking one generation to another. But that brick wall worked both ways. I had difficulty following families into the future through census records. This was not just the challenge of identifying and locating descendants of the people formerly enslaved to my ancestors. Down the decades, I ran into other obstacles that made the search confusing and frustrating. Generational poverty made whole families sink from the record. Post-Reconstruction migration of black families out of a South where racism and lack of opportunity had ground them down, and the changing of names as well as places, all factored into why I couldn't know, and possibly never will know, what happened to the descendants of Moses or Ginette, of the little girl called Satin, of Vinia and her sons.

Still, these challenges were nothing compared to what African American families who want to trace their ancestry run into as a matter of course. For them, the hardest wall of all is tracing back past the 1870 Census, the first one that included people of color as people instead of property. Prior to that, enslaved people were listed by first name and price in inventories, sometimes by given name but more often by sex and estimated age in slave schedules, a kind of addendum to the census listing human property for taxation purposes. If one didn't belong to a remembering family, with letters and affidavits and all the other documentation needed to support family tradition, identifying enslaved ancestors prior to 1870 is sometimes simply impossible.

In a far less significant way, so were my efforts going forward in time. Nina, though, was a woman of deep faith. Not long before her death, in January 2001, she told me, "You will find them. I know you will." What I could scarcely have guessed then, sitting beside my grandmother and reading the copperplate script that gave names and values if not personhood to the black people our ancestors held in bondage, was that when I would one day be able to make contact with descendants of an individual enslaved by our family, it would take me about as far from the cotton fields and scuppernongs and slave cabins of the Deep South as it is possible to go. And that where the search took me, I would also find much that was strangely familiar.

I was born in California, where I lived for the first twenty-eight years of my life, and would only visit the South myself much later. Yet I felt I had a good understanding of what the South was, at least in its surface features, as transmitted through Nina and to a more colorful degree through her mother, Lila.

I never knew the woman who had criticized her husband Charlie for allowing Mr. and Mrs. Daniel to enter the farmhouse by the front door. For a boy like me, Lila was fun to be with. Her likes and dislikes were in the primary colors of childhood, strong and bold, unequivocal. I remember helping her tend her strawberry patch beside her little house in central California. Her strawberries were like fat rubies, laid out at random in the sun-warmed earth which squelched up through my bare feet. Lila held out her calico apron for me to fill with fruit, occasionally wiping the ripest, juiciest ones off on her hip before placing them in my mouth, and laughing. Like children, we shared a few secrets. Once I heard her say the word shit. She'd banged some part of her body on something in the kitchen, and out came the hissed expletive, followed by silence. A moment later, her head, with its crown of cottony white hair, poked around the kitchen door. "You didn't hear that!" she said sharply, though her eyes sparkled in the delicious criminal confidence one child shares with another. Later on, when I was older, I would hear Lila use the word "Negra," or say something dismissive about a person of color, and for the first time noticed how Nina winced. But she said nothing.

To me, though these visits to Nina's family were not in the South, they *were* the South. Lila's daily dramas, so at variance with Charlie's sober, thoughtful silences, the aromas drifting from the kitchen of black-eyed peas with bacon, fried okra (dipped in buttermilk and rolled in cornmeal), collard greens, pepper and salt on everything, and iced sweet tea, all made going to my great-grandparents' house in central California somehow like going back to their—to my—Southern roots. I enjoyed how their household dynamics satisfied expectations founded on Southern stereotypes. At any rate, Lila's and Charlie's little slice of the South in California was as far away as possible from the white winters and blazing autumns of colonial New England, which itself was as far as it was possible to get from the slave cabins and cotton fields of Nina's Southern family history. So it was hard to take in that I was descended from what a genealogist friend of mine jokingly described as the "Congregational aristocracy of Connecticut." But the very first time, and on all subsequent occasions, that I visited New England, it always felt like home.

It was, in a distant way. Through a single ancestral link, a woman born in Connecticut in 1775, my grandmother brought into our Southern gene pool a New England heritage stretching from Revolutionary War officers to *Mayflower* Pilgrims, cousins who signed the Declaration of Independence and others who were activists for abolition.

I shared my love of New England with—perhaps in part derived it from—Nina who, as I've said, had no love for her Southern birthplace. Every month, her issue of *Yankee Magazine* arrived at her California home, and when I was staying with her, Nina and I would sit on the sofa studying the pages. How often we pored over the lovely old New England farmhouses listed (in the early 1970s) for pennies on the dollar in the real estate section, wishing we could buy one. "Wouldn't it be wonderful to live there?" Nina sighed. These houses made Nina recall pieces of antique furniture she had seen as a child, discarded as being "old-fashioned", like the tall case grandfather's clock, which she remembered as being from "back east", sold for a dollar because it was too high to fit into the rooms of her parents' rented farm-house.

Still, in all my research on my Southern ancestors and the people they enslaved, it had not been a priority to look into my New England ancestry. It was comforting knowing I had at least one slender branch on a tree filled with Southerners that was not touched by slavery. But almost a decade after Nina died in 2001, I began to investigate this line, which proceeded from the parents of my fifth great-grandmother, Clarissa Bushnell Baird,[1] born in Connecticut to Eusebius Bushnell and Borodell Latimer, he of Norwich, she of New London.

Norwich, the Bushnells' home town, was laid out on land purchased from Uncas (1588-1683), chief of the Mohegans, and was settled in 1658 by sixty-nine families, of which three, headed by Deacon Thomas Adgate, Samuel Hyde, and Lieut. Thomas Leffingwell, were among Nina's ancestors. (Leffingwell, the author in me was pleased to note, was said to have served as a model for frontiersman Natty Bumppo,

---

[1] Bushnell, George Eleazar, *Bushnell Family Genealogy*, 227-228. Clarissa Bushnell (transcribed incorrectly as "Bushred") married Isham Baird in Nashville, Tennessee on October 21, 1795, by her uncle, Griswold Latimer, who also served as bondsman. (Tennessee State Marriages, 1780-2002, Sumner County, 1787-1838, Microfilm #7). Following their marriage, Isham H. Baird and wife "Claricy" are next mentioned on June 21, 1806, when they sold part of a lot in Lynchburg, Virginia to one Jonathan Mursell (*Lynchburg, VA and Nelson Co. VA (Wills, Deeds and Marriages 1807-1831)* Rev. B. F. Davis, Southern Historical Press, 1985, 49-50). Isham received land grants in Perry County, TN in 1822, 1823 and 1826 (*Tennessee Land Grants*, Book T, page 3, number 16893 & page 13, number 16894; Book W, page 604, number 20966; and Book CC, page 206, number 25057). Their daughter Nancy, born in Tennessee in 1799, married James Shumake and moved with him to Arkansas (Fermine Baird Catchings, *Baird and Beard Families: A Genealogical, Biographical and Historical Collection of Data*, page 120, Group 6-Isham, Nashville: Baird-Ward, 1918).

protagonist of the *Leatherstocking Tales* novels of James Fen-
imore Cooper.) The town's commercial activity was concen-
trated from the beginning around its harbor, formed by the
confluence of the Shetucket and Yantic Rivers with the
Thames, which itself flowed out to the sea. Above this were
softly rolling hills, wooded portions of which were cleared
for farming and homesteads. Arriving somewhat later, the
Bushnells were nonetheless to become a driving force in the
town, not just in business but in civic and religious affairs.

I remember how eager I was to get to Norwich where, as I
found, most of my Bushnell ancestors had lived.[2] The brief
life of David Ruggles, free man of color born in Norwich in
1810, who became one of the fiercest of Abolitionists, had
always intrigued me.[3] Ruggles helped some six hundred fugitive slaves to freedom.[4] Norwich, too, was one of the stops
on the Under-ground Railroad. "Norwich was the terminus
of the Norwich and Worcester railroad line," wrote James
M. Rose and Barbara W. Brown, "by which the Under-

---

[2] "James Ithamar Baird, Arkansas Pioneer," by Dr. Marcus M. Key,
Josie M. Baird and Doss B. Reed, published in Vol. 25, No. 1 of *The
Arkansas Family Historian* (Arkansas Genealogical Society, Russelville,
AR), March 1987, states a Baird family tradition that Clarissa Bushnell
Baird accompanied son James Ithamar Baird to Arkansas, and died in
that state before 1830. A definitive death date and place is not known
for her. Arkansas appealed to members of the Latimer family as well.
Clarissa's uncle, Griswold Latimer, died in Helena, AR, on the border
between Arkansas and Tennessee, in 1829. Another uncle, Wetherell
Latimer, appears in Pope County, AR on September 7, 1837 to apply
for a transfer of his Revolutionary War veteran's pension to his new
residence address (from where he formerly lived in Tennessee.) He died
before the 1840 U.S. Census of Arkansas was recorded. Griswold's and
Wetherell's niece, Ann Latimer Hamilton, also came to Tennessee
where she married, and later removing with her husband to Pope
County, AR.

[3] Finkelman, *The Encyclopedia of African American History*, Vol. 2, 328.

[4] Schneider and Schneider, *Slavery in America*, 454.

ground Railroad of New London County often sent its fugitives to stations in Massachusetts."[5]

There was a quaintness to memories of these ancestors that charmed me, not least because the memories were so imbued with a combined naivety and dry wit I had come to associate with New England, as in colorful information about the family of my ancestor Hannah Griswold Bushnell, in a history written by a descendant, Adeline Bartlett Allyn, and privately published in Hartford in 1908. Adeline drolly repeats sweeping generalizations which occasionally focus on particular personalities, like Hannah Griswold Bushnell's mother, Phebe Hyde Griswold. Phebe, "though probably a beauty", wrote Adeline, "and unquestionably 'Godly', was a careless housekeeper, as she did not air her sheets sufficiently, and thus lost two lovely daughters, one in the bloom of youth and the other in infancy, from the same cause"— which was, Adeline claims, quinsy (infected tonsils), acquired because Phebe put the girls to bed in sheets that had not been sufficiently dried. This account seems rather heartless in laying blame for the girls' deaths squarely on their mother, in times when childhood mortality was high regardless of the state of children's bed sheets. Yet in Adeline's quietly amused narrative, the story took on the stylized outlines of an embroidered sampler. I had a cross-stitch vision of Phebe Hyde Griswold, beautiful, godly and careless, standing at an empty bed, gazing with clasped hands not at the equally culpable unaired sheets but heavenward where, in a blue sky, her daughters' souls joined those other winged spirits, barn swallows or bluebirds, en route way to their divine reward.[6]

---

[5] Rose, *Tapestry*, 45. Norwich had also been home to Aaron Dwight Stevens, hanged in 1860 for his role in John Brown's raid on Harper's Ferry.

[6] Allyn, *Black Hall Traditions* ,40.

These were ancestors with whom, unlike my Southern fore-bears, I felt a oneness, because for me these were people as far removed from slavery as could be imagined. They had lived not on plantations paid for through the free labor of slaves, but in a shining city on a hill.

Or so it seemed.

It is remarkably easy to fall into the folly, and the arrogance, of picking favorites among forebears, like admired charac-ters out of novels or films, based on whatever likable details have been preserved about them over time or those one se-lects as most attractive, and ignoring the ones we would not cross the street to meet. How many enslaver ancestors had I unhappily met in many a crumbling Southern will, alongside the sex, age and value of the people they had enslaved? My eighth great-grandfather, Benajah Bushnell (1681-1762) of Norwich, however, was a relief and a pleasure to encounter. Indeed, he seemed to exemplify everything that I admired about New England.[7]

I wanted to know everything about him, and was lucky to find quite a lot. An inventory of Bushnell's worldly goods, taken at his death, seemed to sketch a deft portrait of a sober, solid, honest man. Among items Benajah Sr. left be-hind were "a Blue Broad Cloth Great Coat", "Silver Shirt Buckel", "one Beaver hat", "Seal'd gold Ring", "one Wigg", "1 Walking Cane", "Silver Sleeve Buttons" and "Silver Bow'd Specticles", along with a quantity of linen shirts and handkerchiefs. I was used to seeing finery of apparel and furnishings in the inventories of my Southern ancestors, no single piece of which could I presume had not been bought

---

[7] Bushnell, *Bushnell Family Genealogy*, 79. I was to later discover that Bushnell played a key role in the colony's efforts to defame Mohegan sachem Mahomet Weyonomon (1700-1736), who sailed to London, and died there shortly afterward, in an attempt to appeal to King George II on behalf of his people, whose lands had been taken by settlers.

without the means produced by slavery. Those were honest threads, the equivalent of fair-trade, non-GMO goods, on old Bushnell's back. I could almost see him, wearing his wig and beaver hat for important meetings in Norwich or Hartford (he represented his town eight times in the General Court) or adjusting his spectacles over accounts (he was chief auditor for the colony) or more pleasant reading material, his silver buttons and shirt buckle sparkling in the transient New England sunshine. He was, as I found, a man who went the extra mile, as when he was investigating a border dispute with Norwich's neighboring settlement of Preston. An old and uncertain Indian land grant overlapped later boundaries, causing confusion for natives and colonists alike. Writing to the Connecticut colony's governor, Joseph Talcott, Benajah Sr. described searching through a cache of papers kept in another community, then emptying his father's "chest" to look for anything relevant there. Finally he went out to the Indian settlement itself to talk to old people who may have preserved memories of the original transaction of the prior century. While there, he noticed and later pointed out to the governor that the wigwams he visited were populated by poor elderly widows, and that the poverty of the settlement in general was such he wished King George II could see it for himself.[8]

And though I am not a religious man myself, I had to admire the energy of Benajah's active devotion. Faith seemed to power all his tangible acts of generosity, along with the belief that there was more good a pair of hands could do than remain constantly pressed together in prayer, which lent a vigorous effectiveness to everything he did.

One night, while Googling for information on Bushnell, I found what at first seemed the best evidence of all for how

---

[8] Inventory of the Estate of Capt. Benajah Bushnell, Vol. 4, 181; Collections of the Connecticut Historical Society, Vol. 4, Hartford 1892, 347-351.

decent a man he was to his fellow man. I had happened upon *The Drock Story*, a research paper produced in August 2003 by Donald W.L. Roddy and Daryl D'Angelo.[9]

The paper referred to a man named Guy Drock who was an employee of my ancestor. "As a boy, and a young man," wrote Roddy and D'Angelo, "Guy worked for Captain Benajah Bushnell, who was a wealthy, influential land speculator...."

> Sometime around 1755, Sarah Powers, a young woman from Newport, on the Colony of Rhode Island, also started working for Benajah Bushnell. We do not know whether Sarah Powers was a voluntary employee of Bushnell or an indentured servant legally obligated to work for him for a specified period of time.... While working for Bushnell, Sarah apparently fell in love with Guy, and probably married him sometime around 1757 or before.... In June, 1759, Guy and Sarah probably stopped working for Benajah Bushnell, and set about trying to make a new life for themselves.[10]

The authors noted that Guy Drock, who was renowned in Norwich as a blacksmith, had a shop not far from where Benajah and Zerviah Bushnell lived. It appeared that in 1773, after both Bushnells had died, their daughter, Mrs. Zerviah Bushnell Holden, sold Guy and Sarah two prime lots—one a quarter of an acre, the other about 1600 square

---

[9] For information on Guy Drock's history and that of his descendants, see Grant Hayter-Menzies, "Slavery and Freedom in a Colonial Connecticut Town," *American Ancestors*, Summer (June) 2012, Vol. 13, Issue 3, 26 (New England Historic Genealogical Society, Boston, MA), which draws on Donald W. L. Roddy and Daryl Y. (Hooper) Holmes, now Daryl D'Angelo, "The Drock Story", Second Edition, August 2005, 28 privately printed by Donald Roddy, no longer available on line.

[10] Holmes [D'Angelo] and Roddy, "The Drock Story", 14.

feet—in the downtown area, one of which included the blacksmith shop, for only £1. Even adjusting for inflation over the course of 240 years, this was a bargain purchase that seemed to me to point to benevolence on part of the Bushnells toward their employees.[11]

It seemed obvious to me what had happened. Bushnell had noticed that his servants, Sarah and Guy, were in love. Playing Cupid in his beaver hat and silver spectacles, Bushnell had not only encouraged his servants to start a life together on their own, but had aided them along the way. The research paper included an inventory of the Drocks' home, taken after Guy's death. With its "great chair", "looking glass", "8 Delph Plates", among the implements of blacksmithing and some kitchenware, the house seemed suffused not just with the love of the couple for one another, but with comforts the Bushnells' kindness had made possible. It was easy to imagine that the expensive dishware had been a wedding present from Bushnell and his wife.

At the top of the page was a facsimile of a deed dating from 1772, but referring to a transaction from June 8, 1759—the year Guy and Sarah Drock set up their own household with the help of Bushnell. Below the facsimile, I read a transcription of the text:

> These may Certify all Persons whom it may Concern that I Benajah Bushnell of Norwich in the County of New London & Colony of Connecticut have sold my Negro Man Named Guy unto her who was called Sarah Powers of Newport on Rhode Island, now called Sarah Drock of Norwich in Connecticut having Received of the Said Sarah Two Years of her Service with some money; for which I acknowledge myself therewith fully Satis-

---

[11] *Ibid.*

fied and Contented and Warrant Secure and Defend the Said Negro to the aforesaid Sarah as being my own proper Estate and free and Clear from any Demands of any Person or Persons Whatsoever: In Witness whereof I have hereunto Set my hand this 8th Day of June 1759 – Benajah Bushnell

In presence of us Joseph Tracy, Benjn Dennis, David Hosmer[12]

"I Benajah Bushnell ... have sold my Negro Man Named Guy unto her who was called Sarah Powers."

Guy Drock was black.

Surely there was some mistake—a first reaction I was to hear echoed by other descendants of New England enslavers.

I sat at my computer for a while after that, re-reading as if somehow another go round would reconfigure the words, change the history, in stark black and white in front of me. Perhaps I had misread, or Roddy and D'Angelo had not transcribed correctly.

I enlarged the image of the deed until it filled the screen. The truth was unavoidable. This was still New England. But it was not a New England I had ever met before.

The image of black slaves in Connecticut ran counter to what I had been taught in school, though I have to say that it rather ran counter to complete silence on the subject. When it came to American history, I and my generation of kids born in the 1960s tended to receive a more or less canned version of our nation's history. I remember only one

---

[12] Norwich Land Records, New London County, Book 19, 374.

class project that touched on the topic of slavery, and I am surprised it took place as early, as best I recall, as the fifth grade. It was a mock debate on the topic of the Dred Scott v. Sandford case of 1857. Our teacher asked us to self select among the different personages involved in the case. Nobody seemed to want John C. Calhoun, so I raised my hand. With my Southern ancestry, it made sense to me. The other kids thought this funny, as the only photos we had seen of Calhoun showed a face of angry cheekbones and hard little eyes under what looked like a silver wig off the head of Phyllis Diller. Then I realized my job would be far from amusing. I had to defend Calhoun's insistence that slaves brought from slave states into free states should in no wise lose their slave status. To the credit of my teacher and the other students, few agreed with my reasoning, which boiled down to the fact that what one owns, whether a cow or a human being, belongs to one, regardless of where one transports it to.

What I remember most clearly of that exercise, however, is that I didn't believe what I was saying. None of the kids in that classroom knew all the ins and outs of the Dred Scott case, but their gut instinct, even at age eleven or so, was that the enslaved man should be freed. I hated playing John C. Calhoun, because I agreed with them, and it showed: in a musty room of a small town elementary school in the foothills of Central California, the Dred Scott decision was overturned. I cheered with my peers, and our teacher suggested we may have just avoided the Civil War. This was heady stuff for children our age, and it was rare. The American history I was taught later on never drew so close to controversy. It was pretty cut and dried.

One of my favorite books in childhood was *The Witch of Blackbird Pond* by Elizabeth George Speare. I loved it because of its com-ing of age plot, but especially because it was set in Connecticut.

Opening in 1687, the story revolves around a teenage girl named Katherine "Kit" Tyler, who leaves the sunny elegance of her late grandfather's bankrupt Barbados estate to come to the gray roofs and gray skies of Wethersfield, Connecticut. There, she seeks refuge with her aunt and uncle, Rachel and Matthew Wood, bringing seven trunks of silk dresses to their "solid and respectable" house, its "clapboards weathered to a silvery gray."[13]

The book is a social justice parable. Kit, brought up cosseted by Barbadian slaves, has to work in Wethersfield onion fields alongside her cousins, and later, no longer the young woman who spoke so blithely of slavery, risks her life to defend an elderly woman accused of witchcraft. Kit needed the crisp air of New England, Speare seems to say, so far distant from the chattel slavery context of her West Indies origins, to develop compassion. The bankruptcy of a Barbadian estate built on slavery, the fact that in order to reach Connecticut at all, Kit has had to sell her personal slave girl for passage money, seem to offer object lessons on the evils of an institution that was just as destructive to the lives of enslavers as it was to the enslaved.

In a heated discussion with Nat Eaton, captain of the ship which had brought Kit to Connecticut, Kit complains about a high smell drifting out of the hold of his vessel, where horses are kept for transport. "Maybe you think it would smell prettier," Nat snarls, "with a hold full of human bodies, half of them rotting in their chains before anyone knew they were dead!" When Kit disbelieves him, Nat tells her about how slaves were transported, and that "to our shame", there were slaves in America, too. Most of them were in Virginia, "But there are plenty of fine folk like you here in New England who'll pay a fat price for black flesh without

---

[13] Speare, *The Witch of Blackbird Pond*, 30.

asking any questions how it got here."[14]

Reading about slaves in Wethersfield in *The Witch of Black-bird Pond*, I had presumed that the author had introduced them as a kind of moral exemplar in the white community of the town, such as often crops up where we least expect it, because everybody knew the only place in America where people owned slaves was in the South. Now I faced a true anomaly to the stereotypes I had cherished of my New England ancestry.

Through my confusion, I knew that before I could understand the conditions under which an upstanding Connecticut gentle-man like Benajah Bushnell could enslave an African man like Guy Drock, I had to teach myself a chapter of American history which had never been revealed to me at school—slavery in early colonial New England—and with it, the history of that institution in a pleasant river town in south-eastern Connecticut. That chapter would become a whole volume, and an absorbing quest.

---

[14] Speare, *The Witch of Blackbird Pond*, 23.

3 THE NORTH DOOR

Thanks to books, documentaries, and that most personal of history courses, tracing my family history, I had acquired what I felt was a reasonable grasp of the facts about the lives of enslaved people in the American South. But what seemed reasonable to me then would come to seem almost criminally deficient in the future.

From these sources I had a sense of what daily life was like for the enslaved, what the expectations were, what more fortunate enslaved people said about what they saw as the benefits of their condition, what the less fortunate remembered of embittering hard labor, punishment, harassment, and general inhumanity during their years as chattel of Southern enslavers. I also had a sense of what their owners were like. Some, like William Ford, first master of kidnapped and enslaved New Yorker Solomon Northup, were remarkably lenient, though not to the degree they were willing to give up the institution altogether. Some Southern slaves, like John Little, who escaped to freedom in Canada, where he was later interviewed for Benjamin Drew's 1856 book *The Refugee; or A North-side View of Slavery*, claimed they were beaten, tortured, starved to the point where it is a wonder they found the strength to live another day, let alone trek over hundreds of miles to where slavery would never threaten them again.

What I did *not* know was what constituted slavery in colonial New England—indeed, I had not yet fully processed the fact that slavery had existed there at all. Yet it turned out information about slavery in the north had been hiding in plain sight all along, much as it had done in the pages of *The Witch of Blackbird Pond*—we just have to know where to look, and most of all, as I would discover, we have to *want* to look for it, a curiosity too often ignored or completely snuffed out by too many Americans today.

"In the eighteenth century," wrote Mary E. Perkins in her magisterial 1895 study of Norwich's historic houses, "there was hardly a Norwich household that did not own one or more slaves."[1] But the institution dated back much further in the colony's history. The first recorded black slave in Connecticut was a man named Louis Berbice, brought by Dutch traders, who died near Hartford in 1639.[2] English colonists were also trying to figure out ways to bring in enslaved blacks to grease the wheels of commerce. In 1645, Emanuel Downing of Rhode Island, brother-in-law of John Winthrop, wrote to Gov. Winthrop that "a war with the Narrangannsett [Indians] is very considerable to this plantation... if upon a just war the Lord should deliver them into our hands, we might easily have men, women and children enough to exchange for Moores [Africans], which will be more gainful pillage for us than we conceive, for I do not see how we can thrive until we get into a stock of slaves sufficient to do all our business."[3] "Slavery was never established in Connecticut by law," writes Daniel Cruson in *The Slaves of Central Fairfield County*. But once it began to take root, Cruson goes on to say, the law had a difficult time removing it, not least because the law protected aspects of keeping slavery in force—slaves were, after all, personal property.[4]

A few years prior to the Revolution, there were an estimated 6,500 African people enslaved in the colony of Connecticut,

[1] Perkins, *Old Houses of the Antient Town of Norwich, 1660-1800*, 127.

[2] Norton, "Negro Slavery in Connecticut" (http://history.rays-place.com/slavery.htm), originally publishaed in *Connecticut Magazine*, Vol. 5, No. 6, June 1899.

[3] Perrault, "Forgotten Voices: A History of Slavery in Saybrook, Connecticut," 9-10.

[4] Cruson, *The Slaves of Central Fairfield County*, 13-14.

a number which dipped to less than half that by the time of the first U.S. census in 1790.[5] According to Connecticut author and historian Frances Manwaring Caulkins, Norwich had a "colored population" larger than that of many towns in the north, but this stood to reason: Connecticut as a whole had one of the largest slave populations in the colonies. "[The Norwich black community] consisted partly of free blacks, accruing from previous occasional manumissions, and partly of persons still held in servitude and bought and sold as property," Caulkins explained.[6]

> From bills of sale that are extant, and from the valuation made in inventories, we learn that in the early part of the century the price for slaves ranged from 60s. to £30.
>
> After this the value increased, and the best were rated at £100. It was not until near the era of the Revolution that the reasonableness and equity of holding the African race in durance began to be questioned by the citizens. At length it was whispered about that it was inconsistent to complain of political oppression, and yet withhold from others the privileges to which they were entitled; to fight for liberty, and yet refuse it to a portion of the human family.[7]

Despite this "portion of the human family" being kept from the freedom that was their birthright, Caulkins claimed that regardless of status, black people were always treated in Norwich "with forbearance and lenity", citing the white community's permission for mock elections of "a negro

---

[5] Cruson, *The Slaves of Central Fairfield County*, 13.

[6] Caulkins, *History of Norwich*, 228.

[7] *Ibid.*, 329.

governor", which "created no little excitement in their ranks."[8]

As proof of lenience toward the enslaved in Norwich, Caulkins points out that in the process of these annual events, African servants took on aspects of the rank and style of their masters, "allowed to use the horses and many of the military trappings of their owners. Provisions, decorations, fruits and liquors were liberally surrendered to them. Great electioneering prevailed, parties often ran high, stump harangues were made, and a vast deal of ceremony expended in counting the votes, proclaiming the result, and inducting the candidate into office,—the whole too often terminating in a drunken frolic, if not a fight."[9]

> It was amusing to see this sham dignitary after his election, riding through the town on one of his master's horses, adorned with plaited gear," Miss Caulkins goes on, "his aids on each side, a la militaire, himself puffing and swelling with pomposity, sitting bolt upright, and moving with a slow, majestic pace, as if the universe was looking on. When he mounted or dismounted, his aids flew to his assistance, holding his bridle, putting his feet into the stirrup, and bowing to the ground before him. The Great Mogul, in a triumphal procession, never assumed an air of more perfect self-importance than the negro Governor at such a time.[10]

But did anyone catch the irony in that election ceremony, in the unaccustomed fanciness of the costumes slaves were allowed to wear for the day, in the masquerade of a fictional vote cast by a powerless electorate, culminating in a crowning and procession which somehow smacked of vaudeville

---

[8] *Ibid.,* 330.

[9] *Ibid.*

blackface of a much later age, albeit played out by actors authentically African?

Among all these histories, familiar names emerged, and with them a first glimpse of my Connecticut ancestors' involvement in the slave trade itself.

Perkins writes of the house belonging to the ancestors of my eighth great-grandmother, Zerviah Leffingwell Bushnell, as "large and rambling, and many parts of it bear the marks of great age.... The entrance door was formerly on the north of the house, and faced the old highway coming down over the hill.... It is said that in early times slave auctions were held at this north door."[10]

Did Guy come to Benajah Bushnell via this door?

Bushnell owned another man, Robin. Robin originally came from the estate of Bushnell's father-in-law, merchant Thomas Leffingwell, on the latter's death in 1724, as part of wife Zerviah's inheritance. Robin appears in the public record first as a slave of Thomas Leffingwell, and again years later as a slave of Benajah Bushnell, and then as a victim of crime. In 1727, Robin was attacked and beaten, it was claimed, by two Indian men, Peter and Tom, whose failure to appear on their court fate was judged admission of guilt.[11]

Leffingwell owned another slave, a woman called Embar. She was described as being "past labor", or too old to work.

---

[10] Perkins, *Old Houses of the Antient Town of Norwich*, 67.

[11] RG 003, New London County Court Native Americans Collection, Nov. 1727, Box 1, folder 29.

This dating could mean that Embar was born sometime in the late 1600s, suggesting she had come directly from Africa or was the child of at least one African parent. Her name may hold a clue. It may possibly be a variant of Amparo— Spanish for "protection"—which brings to mind origins in the Azores, that Portuguese trading floor for slaves from western Africa. She may have been Atlantic creole in origin, what Ira Berlin terms the "Charter Generation" of enslaved people. "Although some of the new arrivals hailed directly from Africa," writes Berlin, "most had already spent some time in the New World, understood the languages of the Atlantic, bore Hispanic and occasionally English names, and were familiar with Christianity and other aspects of European culture." [12]

Where did Embar and Robin live in the Leffingwell house? Thomas Leffingwell's inventory says there was a "kitchin chamber" (a room near the kitchen) containing a bed and, tucked under it, a trundle bed. A combination of imagination and logic suggested to me a scenario for this little room —that Embar, the elder servant who may have nursed generations of Leffingwells, was given the comfortable bed. And Robin, busy boy about the house, slept in the trundle bed in the room with Embar or, more likely, in a hall somewhere outside it. Somehow this image softened the hard edges of why Embar and Robin were living in the Leffingwell house in the first place. How easy to be lulled by that "kitchin chamber", the elderly creole woman and the young boy, the stories she may have told him of the Spice Islands and masters cruel and kind and the sharp sweet tang of sugar cane, so strange to imagine on these cold and remote New England shores. All the best fairytales end with a sting. For all that they were human beings, Embar and Robin sit at

---

[12] Berlin, *Many Thousands Gone*, 29; Thomas Leffingwell Inventory, Case 3167, Probate Files Collection, Early to 1880; Author: Connecticut State Library (Hartford, Connecticut); Probate Place: Hartford, Connecticut.

the bottom of a list on the last page of Leffingwell's inventory, one beginning with fine clothes, jewelry and land, and ending thirty pages later with slaves and livestock, pretty much as my Southern ancestors' inventories did.

What type of enslavers were the Leffingwells, who held slave auctions at the north door of their imposing Norwich residence? One case of conditional manumission seemed to tell a lot about a Norwich businessman named Christopher Leffingwell.

Leffingwell was a son of Benajah Leffingwell, son of Thomas Leffingwell, thus a nephew of my eighth great-grandmother Zerviah Leffingwell Bushnell. He was a well known personage on the stage of colonial America. An early paper manufacturer, Leffingwell supplied the Continental Army with paper cartridges for bullets, was a prominent Stamp Act supporter, and started Connecticut's first chocolate mill.[13] He also owned slaves, one of whom was Romeo.

In this document, dating from October 1778, it is heartening to see that Leffingwell was freeing Romeo, especially during the Revolutionary War, when a case could be made for keeping all the slaves one could to assist with the war effort, if not that a fight said to be based on liberty from the English crown made it a no-brainer to free slaves also. But I looked closer:

> Whereby my late Master Christopher Leffingwell of Norwich, To Whom I was a Servant or Slave during my Natural Life hath this day Emancipated and Set me at Liberty – In Consideration whereof for Value Re-turned of him I hereby promise Engage and agree to do Fifty Faithful Days labour Every year of my Life (if able) for my said Late

---

[13] Perkins, *Old Houses of the Antient Town of Norwich,* 72.

Master, his Heirs & Assigns... to be done at any Season of the year when he or they Call upon me to do it as Witnesseth my Hand in Norwich this First day of October AD 1778.[14]

Romeo didn't sign the document—he made his mark beside the name written for him by clerk John Huntington, member of another slave-owning family of the town. Nor is it clear he understood the contract's obligations. Romeo's "emancipation" reminded me of Guy Drock's. Both were given a "freedom" conditional at best. Guy was free from Benajah Bushnell, but now belonged to his wife. Romeo was freed by Christopher Leffingwell, but for over a month each year, for the rest of his life, with the weak clause "if able", to be interpreted by the Leffingwells rather than Romeo, the former slave was liable to be called to work for this family without pay. In fact, the contract makes it sound as if this work was to be a form of pay off for the freedom Leffingwell claims to have given him. By any definition, that did not seem like freedom to me.

---

[14] New Haven Museum, Leffingwell Family Collection 1698-1888, Manuscripts #25, Box I, Folder D. The document's listing indicates "Order to emancipate C.L.'s slaves, 1778, and a deposition that they will continue to work for family part of each year."

4 TEMPORARY BRETHREN

Benajah Bushnell's slave Guy Drock was definitely a figure in the Norwich community, renowned for blacksmithing skills which would be passed down to several generations of his male descendants. How he came to Norwich and into Benajah Bushnell's ownership is not known. Because he was the first to open the door, as it were, to my New England ancestors' involvement in slavery, I wanted to find out all I could about him.

Guy's first documented appearance was on July 31, 1742, when, "Guy, Servant Boy of Benajah Bushnell," was brought for baptism in Norwich's Congregational Church.[1] The antebellum Southern practice of using the term "boy" for an adult male slave was uncommon in colonial New England; in 1742, Guy probably *was* a boy, with a suggested birth year, per Roddy and D'Angelo, of 1730. If this sample of Norwich's leniency toward its enslaved and free blacks was a world apart from the way blacks were controlled in the South, I could see that merely another version of the same paternalism existed in New England. As in the South, this paternalism was based on the belief that a white master could judge what was best for a slave's body and soul.

Once received into baptism, "Slaves were welcomed into the churches as members where they were assigned to sit with their owner's family or in special pews reserved in the rear for slaves," writes historian Peter Hinks. They became members of a separate community equalized in Christian worship, sometimes seated together with their white masters, but divided by race outside the walls of the place of wor-

---

[1] Norwich First Congregational Church Baptisms, 118 (reproduced in "The Drock Story", 24).

ship. In fact, thus sponsored by paternalism, a slave became more firmly a part of a white family unit controlled by the male head of the household, much as his or her faith in the Christian God made them, on church days, temporary brethren of their white owners.[2]

I wondered whether the high number of slave baptisms in Norwich that spring and summer of 1742 may have been motivated by a Christian revival movement then sweeping all of the colonies. The Great Awakening was all about personal salvation, with emphasis on the concept of individual responsibility—it was as if everyone had been fast asleep, then given a good shaking awake and told, in blinking stupor, that salvation was not just available, but it was the only lifeboat to heaven, and you'd better get in. If the movement awakened, along with moral conscience, a sharpened awareness in some slaveholders that there was something not quite right about holding other human beings in bondage, laying the groundwork for manumissions (many of them conditional), in others it may simply have activated a sense of paternalistic duty to their enslaved people, for whose souls as well as bodies they were responsible. And it may be that the Great Awakening, for these and perhaps other reasons far too obscure to guess at, motivated Benajah Bushnell to have Guy baptized in the Christian faith.[3]

Finding the right kind of faith—rather, to pose an anachronistic simile, like turning the dial of a radio to locate the clearest signal—seems to have been of interest to my ancestor Benajah Bush-nell, to such degree he switched allegiance from the Congregational to the Episcopal church. According to Caulkins, between 1742 and 1750 Captain Bushnell

---

[2] Hinks, "Citizens All: African Americans in Connecticut 1700-1850": http://cmi2.yale.edu/citizens_all/stories/module1/documents/pdfs/mod_1_digging_deeper.pdf , 6.

[3] Glasson, *Mastering Christianity*, 38.

and several prominent Norwich citizens raised funds to erect an Episcopal church on land that was donated by Bushnell for that specific purpose. They were a little late in the game: episcopacy had arrived in Connecticut in 1722, writes Caulkins, "though it was first introduced by the Rev. Mr. Muirson, a missionary from the 'Society for the Propagation of the Gospel in foreign parts', at Stratford [CT], in 1706." But where religious faith was concerned, it was likely considered a case of better late than never. Bushnell's switch may have had something to do, too, with his status as slaveholder.[4]

The Society for the Propagation of the Gospel, known by the shorthand of SPG, was founded in 1702. Its charter mandated evangelization among slaves and Native American peoples in the colonies. Those who were members of the SPG believed that slaves' humanity ought to be respected, and yet in keeping with a powerful Calvinist notion of predestination, according to which some are saved and others not, most SPG fathers insisted that God had clearly ordained some human beings to serve and others to rule; it was no mortal man's place to interfere in what the Creator had devised. Thus could the SPG justify slavery on Codrington Plantation, the organization's estate in Barbados, where with an irony that still takes the breath away, Christianized slaves were branded on the chest with the word "Society" so as to be immediately identifiable should they escape.[5]

I could not find any evidence for or against their membership in the SPG, but Benajah Sr. and Zerviah clearly supported the Society with their pocketbook. Five years after Benajah's death in 1762, his widow would make over land to

---

4 Caulkins, *History of Norwich*, 261-263.

5 Glasson, *Mastering Christianity*, 104–105.

the organization for a house for the SPG missionary—a clear case of sympathy for the SPG's values.[6]

No one knows Sarah Powers' ethnicity. Yet while Guy is always referred to as "Negro Man, Guy," Bushnell's reference to Sarah is what it would be for any white individual—i.e., there is no mention of ethnicity whatsoever. Seventeen years after Bushnell brought Guy into the fold of his church, he sold him to Sarah, whose presence in the Bushnell household and in Norwich remains a mystery. Was she also employed by the Bushnells, or elsewhere in town? How did she meet Guy? We can only surmise. What I did find, however, is that a free white woman having a relationship with a black slave in colonial Connecticut was not unknown. Lemuel Haynes (1753–1833) was born in Hartford to a slave father and white indentured servant mother. As a preacher, Haynes advocated harmony between the races, and lived his precepts by marrying a white woman (who had proposed to him).[7]

Interestingly, Guy's sale was not the end of the relationship between the Bushnells and Drocks. Guy's house and blacksmith shop stood on Bushnell property, near the lot Zerviah had deeded to the SPG. It will be recalled that after Zerviah's death in 1770, her daughter Zerviah Holden sold the land to Guy and Sarah for a mere £1. And a new generation of Bushnell descendants assisted a new generation of Drocks. In 1788, a year after Guy's death, his son Simon purchased property in Newport, New Hampshire, from Isaac Tracy, Jr., Captain Bushnell's grandson.[8]

---

[6] Caulkins, *History of Norwich*, 453.

[7] Taylor et al., "BlackPast.org, Remembered & Reclaimed": biography of Rev. Lemuel Haynes: www.blackpast.org/?q=aah/haynes-lemuel-1753-1833.

[8] Holmes [D'Angelo] and Roddy, "The Drock Story," 14-15.

The Drock Story gave me some idea of the family's later history after the lifetimes of Guy's children. A few generations later, a branch of the family began giving out information, undoubtedly in response to persistent inquiry and perhaps prejudice as well, that the Drocks were of Native American descent. They were assisted in this effort at "passing" for white by what appear to be deliberate marital choices. "It seems there must have been several white spouses in the Drock line," write Roddy and D'Angelo, "because by around 1840 and after, a rather large proportion of the Drock descendants were light enough to occasionally pass for white." After the Civil War, more transformations took place among Guy Drock's descendants. "Nearly all of those with the Drock surname eventually modified the spelling and pronunciation of the name, some of them becoming DeRock, others Derock, and still others De Roque. Without exception these new families blended into white communities," sometimes alluding, as they had once done to Indian ancestry, to origins in France or Spain.[9]

Daryl D'Angelo summed this up by explaining that "The Drocks and related families functioned as *isolates*. That is, they lived as a group that was essentially isolated from the larger community around them. The reason for this isolation can easily be explained by the racial prejudices that have existed in our culture since the early days of slavery." She added that she was aware of black and mixed race Drock descendants still living in New York State who were aware of branches of the family who had crossed the color line; significantly, they did not know them.[10]

The most compelling fact I learned from Donald Roddy and Daryl D'Angelo's research paper was that *they* were descendants of Guy Drock.

---

[9] *Ibid.*, 20.

[10] *Ibid.*, 20-21.

I, who had pored over post-Civil War census records, posted letters and emails, in hope of finding descendants of people my Southern ancestors had enslaved, had stumbled over the history and mystery of slavery in New England. In the process, I had all but walked right up to descendants of an African man my Connecticut ancestor had enslaved over a century before the outbreak of the Civil War.

5 NERO, CESAR, JUBA AND ROSE

From my research into my Southern ancestry, I was used by now to seeing enslaved people in the inventories of quite ordinary people—planters who could barely write their name or who could not write at all; who could read, after a fashion, but left a single book, the family Bible, in their wills, and who showed few signs of having more than a rudimentary education. (This refers mostly to male ancestors; many of the women seem not only to have been literate but to have written with a fine hand.) And among my Southern ancestors, nobody I knew of had been a preacher, a mayor, a judge.

This journey into my New England ancestry was to change that impression vividly. I would find highly literate businessmen like Benajah Bushnell and Thomas Leffingwell. And I would find those professionals, including clergy, in whose households I found it difficult to imagine slaves, with that prejudiced view that only the rural and uneducated could justify slavery. This would be another lesson learned.

My eighth great-grandfather John Griswold (1690-1764) was known as "Judge" John from his many years of service as a justice of the peace in Lyme. "He was not only a gentleman of great wealth," ran the sermon spoken at his funeral, "but much esteemed by his townsmen and acquaintances for his superior wisdom and integrity."[1] Judge John also owned at least four African slaves, a woman named Phillis, a boy named Neptune, whom the Judge brought to baptism in 1741 (a year before the Bushnells brought Guy Drock), and two unnamed males.[2]

---

[1] Allyn, *Black Hall Traditions,* 41.

[2] Salisbury, *The Griswold Family in Connecticut,* 152; Brown & Rose, 539.

Where Judge John's wife's family was concerned, slavery would play a much more substantial role—indeed, would rank them among the more infamous slave traders of history.

Judge John married Hannah Lee, daughter of Thomas Lee and Mary DeWolf. Mary's grand-nephew was Charles Nathan DeWolf, born in Lyme in 1695, died in West Africa in 1726. Charles Nathan's son, Mark Antony DeWolf, married Abigail Potter, sister of "the first captain from Bristol [Rhode Island] to invest in transporting Africans to the Caribbean and the southern colonies."[3] Mark Antony DeWolf joined his brother-in-law and, as author Thomas DeWolf explains, "The generation of Mark Antony DeWolf's grandchildren was the third, and last, to be broadly involved in the [slave] trade, with business interests in New England, plantations in Cuba, and an auction house in South Carolina."[4] In fact, the DeWolfs, based out of Bristol, had made themselves the richest slave-trading family in America. "Theirs was one of the few fortunes that truly rested on rum and slaves," writes Prof. Jay Coughtry. "In the annals of the American slave trade, the deWolfs are without peer."[5]

As with the DeWolfs, slavery seemed to be passed along in my other New England family lines, like a kind of calling, from father to son or, in certain cases, father-in-law to son-in-law. Judge John's son, Rev. George Griswold, was the father of Lucretia Griswold, who married my seventh great-grandfather Col. Jonathan Latimer and migrated with him from Connecticut to Tennessee after the War of Indepen-

---

[3] DeWolf, *Inheriting the Trade*, 42-43.

[4] *Op. cit.*, Family Tree, VIII.

[5] Farrow, Lang, and Frank, *Complicity*, 111.

dence.[6] In 1730, Rev. Griswold, well-respected spiritual leader of his community, purchased a "Negro woman" named Cornelia from Joseph Coit of New London.[7]

For a tradition of slavery through generations, however, I found that Rev. Griswold's wife, Hannah Lynde, came from a family where slaves were to be found in four generations of the same family.

In fact, the Lyndes were not just the earliest enslavers in my ancestry—among the earliest in Massachusetts—but were, after the DeWolfs, among the most extensive New England enslavers I had yet discovered in my bloodline.

Hannah's father was Nathaniel Lynde. Born in Boston in 1659, one of seven sons (out of eleven children total) of land speculator and, later, judge, Simon Lynde, one of Boston's most prominent citizens, Nathaniel Lynde was indeed a golden boy of colonial New England. At 24, he married Susannah Willoughby, daughter and heiress of Francis Willoughby, Deputy Governor of the Massachusetts colony, and wife Margaret Locke Taylor, rich widow of a London merchant and great-granddaughter of a London merchant, Thomas Locke, who brought captive Africans up the River Thames in 1555, the first ever seen in London.[8]

After Nathaniel had apprenticed in business with his father, Simon gave the young couple large tracts of land he owned in and around Saybrook, hugging the southeast coast of

---

[6] Walworth, *Hyde Genealogy*, 192.

[7] Brown & Rose, *Black Roots in Southeastern Connecticut*, 539.

[8] Lynde, *The Diaries of Benjamin Lynde and of Benjamin Lynde Jr.*, vii; Chester, "The Descent of Margaret Locke, Third Wife of Deputy Governor Francis Willoughby," 59-65; Wise, *Though the Heavens May Fall*, 16.

Connecticut. There the couple took up residence, producing ten children. Nathaniel seems to have lived out the quiet life of a country gentleman, looking after his lands and involving himself in civic affairs. We know he took a serious interest in education. In 1701, he served as first treasurer of the Saybrook Collegiate School, embryo of what became Yale University, and he donated the land for the school. This donation included the proviso that the school must remain in Saybrook. When it did not, removing to New Haven in 1716, the land reverted back to Nathaniel.[9]

At his death in 1729, nineteen years after the death of Susannah, two plain sandstone memorial tablets were raised to husband and wife in a section of what is now Cypress Cemetery, looking past the mouth of the Connecticut River to the Atlantic Ocean. Undecorated though these gravestones may have been, the glitter that was this couple's life shows in an inventory filled with silverware and jewelry—sterling salt cellars, a pearl necklace valued at the princely sum of £40, diamond clasps and sealing wax, and silver-set "coconut cups", the latter a bibelot that became fashionable with the island trade, not just in the colonies but in England and elsewhere.[10]

Half a humble coconut polished up and given a foot-stool of silver reminded me of those portraits fashionable at the time, in which black slaves were shown garbed in rich satins, bending low with a tray for a white milady. So it was when we got the taste for sugar, for pepper, for exotic comestibles like bananas and coconuts. And for slaves. This was underscored when I found four Africans listed alongside these other tangible riches: Nero, Cesar, Juba, and a woman, Rose, a floral sobriquet associated with French serving-maids and

---

[9] Lynde, *The Diaries of Benjamin Lynde* , vii-viii.

[10] Salisbury, *The Griswold Family* , Vol. 1, Part 2, 400-401.

hairdressers, which is possibly the service Rose provided for Mistress Lynde.[11]

Four slaves was considered a large number for an early eighteenth century New England household. In the latter seventeenth century, that number of enslaved people was usually the most that could be imported from Barbados.[12]

Coastal Saybrook, where the wealthy Hart family owned female slaves "wearing white and parti-colored turbans... dropping curtsies as they entered and left a room", was a place where a successful blacksmith could own nine human beings, each with his or her name smacking of Greece, Rome and the Old Testament. But not every Saybrook enslaver was like Samuel Lynde, Nathaniel's son. Like the Lyndes in general, Samuel in particular was in a class all his own.[13]

A graduate of the Collegiate School, Samuel served as a judge, like his Boston grandfather, and like him had a hand in virtually everything that was anything in the region where he lived. He was a learned man, leaving a library of 250 books. He was also an important cog in the engine that served the West Indies trade. Livestock and produce he raised on his farms provided places like Barbados, unable to provide for themselves, the basics of life, directly supporting all aspects of West Indies business, including, indirectly, slavery. Samuel also had a more direct connection to slavery. Through a home-based factory for spinning and weaving,

---

[11] *Ibid.*, Part 2, 400.

[12] Perrault, "Forgotten Voices," 23.

[13] *Ibid*, 37, 38.

his household of nine slaves was kept so busy at wheel and loom they made him rich even by Boston standards.[14]

Just four females among these enslaved people were responsible for one of the most substantial cottage industries anywhere in the Lower Connecticut River valley.[15] Ironically, the cloth and the finished garments these women wove and sewed in an attic served the West Indies, like the pork and vegetables off Samuel's farmlands.

It came as no surprise to me that Samuel's grandfather, Simon Lynde, owned African slaves. What I was not prepared for was undeniable proof of his complicity in some of the worst aspects of the slave trade itself—the bartering of one race of people for ownership of another.

---

[14] *Ibid*, 42-43.

[15] *Ibid*, 46.

6 BRUISED REEDS

Born in London in 1624 to a Dutch shipping merchant and a daughter of fallen English gentry, Simon Lynde was a unique amalgam of tycoon and gentleman.

An eager go-getter who amassed property across several American colonies, Simon married the daughter of a wealthy Boston haberdasher, and lived in Boston's Beacon Hill neighborhood. Very much the prototype of the wide-ranging, not particularly scrupulous American businessman, Simon also never forgot his mother's aristocratic origins or her family connections to the royal court. A year after Charles I was beheaded and England fell under control of Cromwell, Simon, who had been presented to the king as a boy, left England for the New World, and apparently never went back. He had found a theatre for unlimited business development, and he had also found a way to restore in America what his mother's family had lost in England.[1]

Simon's mother, Elizabeth Digby (?-1669), was a grand-daughter of Simon Digby of Bedale, a landed gentleman with marble ancestral effigies and noble and royal forebears behind him. In the 1569 Northern Uprising, Digby forfeited estate and life; with other captured men, he was drawn and quartered at York, and his head mounted on the battlements.[2]

This was a loss to the family not merely of their paterfamilias but of their lands and thus source of income, and a significant social setback. But Simon's granddaughter, Elizabeth

---

[1] Weis and Sheppard, *Ancestral Roots of Certain American Colonists*, 96.

[2] S *Ibid.*, 96.

Digby Lynde, who married Anglo-Dutch London merchant Enoch Lynde, ambitiously kept up with her more prominent cousins. Through one of them, John Digby, Earl of Bristol, Elizabeth managed to have young Simon presented to King Charles I, whose hand the young boy kissed at court. Perhaps Elizabeth believed this an opening for her son to have a place at court or in some office bestowed by the king. If there were such plans, Charles's downfall put paid to them.[3]

Clearly, for Simon, from an early age his mother's remote past of vanished family estates and sought-after noble kinships was there to offset his father's pragmatic commercial present. Named for the maternal great-grandfather who had lost everything, perhaps Simon set himself to get it all back and then some in what was known to Europeans as the "New World", where the primary source of wealth was land which lay virtually free for the picking, provided one knew how to obtain it cheaply from its Indian stewards. He was not alone in this quest. Like Governor John Winthrop Simon would join other prominent settlers in recreating "the manors of their former homeland with retinues of Indian dependents," who were typically enslaved.[4]

One of Simon's friends and business associates in Massachusetts, Major Humphrey Atherton (circa 1608-1661), was a busy exploiter of these native peoples. A persecutor of Quakers and a player in the 1654 witchcraft trial and execution of Boston matron Ann Hibbins.[5] Atherton was an especially stark example of the ambitious white man indige-

---

[3] Lynde, *The Diaries of Benjamin Lynde,* vi.

[4] Lynde, *op. cit..*,vi; Salisbury, 374; Newell, *Brethren by Nature,* 9.

[5] Ann Hibbins was the widow of William Hibbins, who conducted the marriage ceremony of Simon Lynde and Hannah Newgate on February 22, 1652. See *Documents of the City of Boston,* Vol. 3, 38, Boston City Council, Boston: Rockwell and Churchill, 1884.

nous peoples (and all strong-minded women) had to contend with. Through "Indian purchases", in which lands were alleged by Atherton to have been gifts from chiefs "for loue and affection", Atherton and partners—among them Simon Lynde—obtained large swathes of real estate throughout Massachusetts, Connecticut and Rhode Island for virtually nothing, profiting themselves and their heirs at the expense of the original inhabitants.[6] Fortunes were ripe for the picking for men like Simon Lynde, but sometimes the hunger for land and profits forced white men like him to commit deeds that could be "justified" neither by questionable deals or by Indian aggression. And as with the way settler speculators went about obtaining native land, there were also various ways to go about obtaining people. This is where the most unsavory of Simon's activities come into focus.[7]

In Dover, Maine on August 27, 1676, during the upheaval of King Philip's War, when Indians merely deemed a threat were regularly taken captive, four men came before Commissioners Thomas Gardner and Richard Oliver to report concerns about a ketch called the *Endevor*.

The ketch, they said, belonged to Simon Lynde of Boston. The men testified that they had been alerted by a Frenchman at Mt. Desert that *Endevor*, leased by Henry Lawton and

---

[6] White, *American Indian Chronology*, 28. Major Richard Waldron carried on this tradition decades later during King Philip's War (in 1676, the year *Endevor* sailed to the Azores): see Newell, "Indian Slavery in Colonial New England" in *Indian Slavery in Colonial America* (Lincoln: University of Nebraska Press, 2010), 50-51; Hilden, "Hunting North American Indians in Barbados", http://realhistoryww.com/world_history/ancient/Misc/Barbados/Hunting_North_American_Indians_in_Barbados.htm. For Anne Hibbins, see Simons, *Witches, Rakes, and Rogues*, 7-15.

[7] Martin, *Profits in the Wilderness: Entrepreneurship and the Founding of New England* (Chapel Hill: University of North Carolina Press, 1991) 58-59 and 62-64.

John Laverdure, with merchant William Waldron aboard, "did carry 9 Indians away from Michias [sic] and more from Cape Sables." Thomas Gardner was perhaps unique among traders in desiring peace with the native tribes of Maine. When he had first been informed that there were shackles on *Endevor*, Gardner "wrote a letter to the master and company at Monhegan [on the southern Maine coast] warning them not to take any Indians east side of the Kenibek river because we had made peace with them."[8]

Henry Lawton had been granted this license to kidnap by Major Richard Waldron (1615–1689), president of colonial New Hampshire, who was to play a bloody role in Indian-settler relations and himself come to a bad end at their hands. This "permit" enabled Lawton to take captive "all the Indians 'of the East' who so far had been plundering towns and villages," though the real plunder was what was taking place on the *Endevor*. After leaving Maine, the *Endevor* sailed north to Cape Sable, just as the Mt. Desert Frenchman had reported, where Laverdure enticed several more Indians (possibly Mi'kmaq) aboard by speaking their language and feeding them. Some seventeen were duped in this manner, including the chief and his wife. The crew and their human loot then sailed east, where all were sold at Faial.[9]

There is reason to believe that this *Endevor* was the "barque" of the same name built in New London, Connecticut by the firm of Mould & Coit in about 1660 for Capt. Matthew Beckwith (1610-1680). Beckwith was in the Barbados trade, that nexus for sugar, rum and slaves, and was not only Si-

---

[8] Noyes et al., *Genealogical Dictionary of Maine and New Hampshire* (Baltimore: Genealogical Publishing Company, 2002), Massachusetts Archives lxi, 73, 4 (Suffolk Court Files 1592).

[9] Borque, *Twelve Thousand Years*, 153-154; d'Entremont, "He Jumped Bail", *Yarmouth Vanguard*, April 11, 1989 (http://www.museeacadien.ca/english/archives/articles/15.htm).

mon's brother-in-law but was the father of Prudence Beck-with, who married into the slave-trading DeWolf family. In 1666, Beckwith sold *Endevor* in Barbados for 2000 pounds of sugar. From there, it may have made its way into Simon Lynde's hands.[10]

Barbados was familiar territory to Simon: it had been his first stop as a young voyager to Boston from London in 1650, because he witnessed there a will for a rich landowner and possible relative named Colonel Christopher Lynd who, unlike ordinary folks whose smaller debts Simon would be quick to collect, still owed his estate a great deal of money—as did John Drax of the Barbados sugar fortune—at Lynde's death in 1687. Born around 1642, Drax died a bachelor in 1671. He was a son of Sir James Drax, one of the first English emigrants to Barbados and founder of the family's sugar empire. From its origins as a domesticated crop in New Guinea, sugar cane became what historian Matthew Parker aptly terms "white gold", a crop which occasioned difficulty along every stage of its processing, under conditions requiring an army of enslaved people whose lives were counted in a matter of months, but with a huge profit at the end for the plantation owner.[11]

Sugar was the sort of solid investment Simon Lynde might have been attracted to—we know he owned an interest in a

---

[10] "Captain Matthew Beckwith" (posted May 14, 2010): http://min-erdescent.com/2010/05/14/matthew-beckwith/. There may be a Simon Lynde family connection with Matthew Beckwith: Beckwith is said to have married a sister of Lynde's named Elizabeth. *Torrey's New England Marriages Prior to 1700*, Clarence Almon Torrey, 2487 (Boston : New England Historic Genealogical Society, 1971), shows Beckwith's wife Elizabeth/Mary as (LYNDE?). Newell (*Brethren by Nature*, 202) writes, "The *Endeavor*, built in New London by the family of its captain, John Haughton, had earlier transported slaves in the Barbados trade."

[11] Brandow, *Genealogies of Barbados Families*, 414; *Suffolk Deeds*, Vol. XIV, 345, 346.

"plantacion" located in the parish of St. Michael, at the southern end of Barbados, near Bridgetown. We do not know, but is not impossible that this property came to him through the common practice of seizing valuables when the debtor could not pay, perhaps from John Drax or another overextended family of rich Barbados planters. It may well be that the "ffour Negros" later listed in his Boston inventory became Lynde's property via the same means.[12]

To give him the benefit of the doubt, is certainly possible that Simon did not know to what uses *Endevor* was put in 1676. Lawton and Laverdure were only leasing the ship; given what we know of their characters, they may have failed to disclose what they planned to do with it. We do not know the details of the contract they had with Simon. Yet it is unlikely that Lawton, Laverdure and Waldron were authorized to keep *all* the proceeds from sale of their cargo, human or otherwise. The barque's owner would have been entitled to a share of whatever profits the lessees obtained, and thus would be more likely than not to know how they had obtained them. And in this very year, Simon was one of the more significant purchasers of Indian slaves at a vast Massachusetts Bay Colony auction, "buying Indians for [his] own use and for export." Besides all this, there were other witnesses implicating Simon in transatlantic slave traffic.[13]

---

[12] *Suffolk Deeds*, Vol. IV, 43, 44; *Suffolk County, MA, Probate Records*, Volumes 10-12, 1687-1697, volume 10, 188-193. Nathaniel Lynde, first treasurer of Saybrook Collegiate School (precursor to Yale University), staffed his household in Old Saybrook with four African slaves, Rose, Juba, Cesar and Nero. If the four slaves listed in Simon Lynde's inventory in 1687 were young people at the time, these could well be the same ones, inherited by his son. In this family, the tradition of slavery descended to the third generation, with Nathaniel Lynde's son Samuel using his female slaves Jenny, Zina, Phillis and Lilly to run a homegrown cloth business that helped him accrue sizable wealth.

[13] Newell, *Brethren by Nature,* 191.

In *The History of the Indian Wars in New England*, Rev. William Hubbard (1621-1704) notes two eyewitness accounts of Boston ships carrying Indian slaves to Faial. In mid-November 1676, one Thomas Miller deposed that "being at Feall [Faial] he met with a Vessel which had come in some seven or eight days before [November 4] which, on Inquiry he learned was from 'Bosting' [Boston]... Saw Indians on board but how many he could not tell....He further learned they were gotten at the Eastward, and that the Vessel [Ketch] belonged to Mr. 'Lines'." Around this same time, two other men reported they had seen in Faial "sometime the last Aprill [1676]...a small Ketch there which came from New England and had severall Indians aboard." There may have been as many as twenty captives. The men could not remember the name of the ship or of the master, but they did discover "the Ketch was Mr. Line's and belonged to Boston."[14]

As a prominent Boston merchant, "Mr. Line" would have been well known across the Atlantic. "Line" was a spelling (perhaps influenced by pronunciation) often used at this time for the Lynde surname. If Simon Lynde was duped by Lawton and company as to their use of his ship, and found —as his reputation for moral high ground would lead us to suspect—that this use was against his principles, we would expect him to press charges. But he does not appear to have done so. In the end, Laverdure's mother freed him on bail (and he proceeded to run for it, later changing his name), and though jailed, Lawton and Waldron were acquitted. Simon Lynde emerged with reputation unscathed.[15]

---

[14] Hubbard, *The History of the Indian Wars in New England*, xix

[15] 15 Lillis, "Forging New Communities: Indian Slavery and Servitude in Colonial New England 1676-1776", 46-47; d'Entremont: http://www.museeacadien.ca/english/archives/articles/15.htm

Simon died a wealthy man, the paterfamilias of a brood of successful children, who specified bequests to unborn grand-children, though the debts of people he knew to be "desperate" were not stricken from his books at his death.[16] In his will, he wrote that though "I have In no measure rendered unto the Lord according to mercies received, yet looking towards his holy Temple and Reposing in his mercies and merits who Delights to forgive...I trust and cast my Self upon him who will not quench the Smoaking flax nor break the bruised Reed." The imagery comes from the Bible: "A bruised reed shall he not break, and smoking flax shall he not quench, till he send forth judgment unto victory" (Isaiah 42)—underscoring Simon's hope that his Savior will take pity on all his faults; not break the twisted reed or snuff out the smoldering lamp but recognize them as proofs, if faltering, of devoted faith. The implication is that unnamed sins continued to weigh on Simon at the end, though in truth many wills orchestrate contrition in this manner. It is an ironic valediction for a man who played a role in casting Indian slaves upon shores thousands of miles from their homeland, a man whose African slaves in Boston surely could have told their master all about how it felt to be a bruised reed.[17]

---

[16] *Suffolk County, MA, Probate Records*, Volumes 13-14, 1688-1701, volume 13, 153.

[17] *Suffolk Deeds*, Vol. IV, 43, 44; Suffolk County, MA, Probate Records, Volumes 10-12, 1687-1697, volume 10, 188-193.

7 COMING TO THE TABLE

The weight of the ancestral legacy I had discovered had become too massive for me to carry alone. I had to talk about it with people who could help me make sense of it. Which is why I, in September 2011, waited on the other end of a conference call with members of Coming to the Table (CTTT).

Founded in 2006, CTTT arose out of a gathering at Eastern Mennonite University in Harrisonburg, Virginia, and was first suggested by Susan Hutchison, a white descendant of Thomas Jefferson, and by Will Hairston, whose Southern ancestors enslaved many hundreds of African American people. Hairston's family history was the subject of *The Hairstons: An American Family in Black and White* by historian Henry Wiencek, and it was Wiencek, significantly, who put Hutchison and Hairston in touch with one another. "Together, they came up with the idea of a family reunion that was vastly different from what most people are accustomed to," writes Thomas DeWolf. "It would not be a meeting of just one family. It would be a reunion that involved multiple families from both sides of the racial construct; a re-union of black and white—the descendants of people who were slaveholders with the descendants of those they had enslaved." Out of this uncertain beginning, the idea of Coming to the Table was born. Staff at The Center for Justice & Peacebuilding at Eastern Mennonite University came on board to locate grant funding and eventually to take on all responsibilities for keeping CTTT financially viable, and assisted in developing the CTTT approach, leading training sessions in the Transforming Historical Harms (THH) model for descendants, black and white, of American slavery.[1]

---

[1] DeWolf and Morgan, *Gather at the Table*, 6.

I was curious about and moved by the concept of historical harms, which put into words the inchoate mass of impressions that flooded me, and which appeared to offer tools for how to deal with them in a way that would provide clarity and, possibly, reconciliation between me and my family history, and perhaps reconciliation between me and the descendants of people my family had enslaved. It helped greatly to be able to put a name to what I felt about what historical slavery has done to both the descendants of the enslaved and the descendants of the enslavers—those, that is, among the latter who want to know the truth. Even with a handle to hang on to, I just didn't realize how difficult it would be to talk to other people about my family history. On that first conference call from my home in British Columbia, I was glad my fellow participants couldn't see the frantic notes I was scribbling myself as I waited for all the callers to ping in: "What are you doing? What is this about? What do you have to offer? What is this past to you?"

But it was everything to me. I could not understand how my ancestors had lived their daily lives knowing that the entire structure of their material existence—from their habitual activities to their furniture and china, silverware and side-saddles, livestock and cotton gins—was supported by slave labor. It was easy to feel anger. But was it useful? What I struggled with was what to do with what continued to feel, to me, the abiding responsibility for what to do with their legacy, and how to make it something positive, something that offered change to problems in our current world that were the heirs of slavery and racism, much as I was the heir to enslavers and racists. What made broaching this conversation even more complicated for me was the two new genealogical discoveries I had recently made, each a challenge to unpack so that I, let alone anybody else, could understand and learn from what I'd found.

Grandson of Benajah Bushnell of Norwich (enslaver of Guy Drock), my sixth great-grandfather Eusebius Bushnell was born in Norwich in 1747, and died in Florida around 1812. Eusebius served as officer in the War of Independence, married his cousin, Borodell Latimer, and left Connecticut for greener pastures. A land speculator by trade, Eusebius had moved often (sometimes to keep ahead of the law), but most of his activity was in Tennessee and in Florida, where he owned, among other business ventures, a sawmill near St. Augustine and a tanning yard in the city.[2] It was there he, scion of generations of Protestant New England Puritans, converted to Catholic faith on December 5, 1806.[3] For what reason he did this nobody knows, but what startled me was his choice of godfather.

The fifty-nine year old Eusebius Bushnell took the name Fernando in honor of Don Fernando de la Maza y Arredondo (born 1765 in Spain). Of the thousands of Florida acres that were his, Don Fernando is now mostly remembered for having helped raise a monument on the Plaza de la Constitucion in 1813, commemorating Spain's constitution granted in that year. However, the Plaza de la Constitucion is known for another landmark and a far older one: St. Augustine's slave market, which dates to 1598. Slavery and Don Fernando were closely related, because Don Fernando was one of the most infamous of early nineteenth century transatlantic slave traders. In August 1810, Don Fernando's slave ship, *Sevilla*, sailed with a cargo of 174 African slaves, its destination Amelia Island off the Florida coast. Amelia Island was preferred because the United States government had outlawed the transatlantic slave trade in 1808. Being under control of Spain, Florida was immune from American laws.

---

[2] Bushnell, *Bushnell Family Genealogy*, 227-28.

[3] St. Augustine Genealogical Society web site: http://www.stauggens.com/stJohnsRecords/churchRecords/SACBaptf.html.

By the time the *Sevilla* arrived, twenty-eight slaves were dead (a mortality rate of 17%). Just transporting enslaved people from the African coast to these ships was a nightmare by itself. Marcus Rediker writes of the trauma of Africans captured for black and white slavers with the connivance of local tribes, the marches in coffles to where the ship waited at the coast, the Gola warriors who, "enslaved by force...in capture, or through judicial punishments in their society of origin" fought to the death to get out of their shackles, while those that survived this had an ocean voyage to endure and, if they did, the future ordeals of being paraded at auction and worked at the pleasure of white masters. Many of Arredondo's human cargo were sick but still breathing; Arredondo, however, proved himself master of the discount. "Fifty-five slaves were so ill," writes historian Jane Landers, "that Arredondo sold them for between fifty and one hundred pesos." Nine slaves were so sick nobody would buy them. With his proceeds, Don Fernando purchased Florida cotton and pine wood, which was sold to the United States and England in a nineteenth century version of the Triangle Trade.[4]

My questions about my ancestor were many. The most cogent, for me, however, was the question of whether Eusebius was also a slave trader or involved in the business of his godfather. It seemed very likely he was.

My other discovery stretched farther back in time, but its impact was that of an event much closer to me. I had been reading Steven M. Wise's book *Though the Heavens May Fall: The Landmark Trial That Led to the End of Human Slavery*, about the famous 1772 Mansfield Judgment. That year, England's chief jurist, Lord Mansfield, ruled in favor of an enslaved man named James Somerset, who had been brought

---

[4] Landers, *Black Society*, 176-177; Rediker, 73-75.

to England by his Boston-based master and petitioned the Lord Chief Justice for his freedom.

In the beginning of Wise's book, the name of one John Lok, merchant, caught my eye. In 1555, Lok brought what are believed to be the first native Africans to London. These were five Ghanaian men—Anthonie, George, Binne (apparently a Hausa word referring to a dry period for sowing before rainy season), and two whose names are not known—whom Lok brought in his trading ship from the west coast of Africa, men who shared space on board with those other commodities of quick cash, ivory, gold and spices. I noted this name because it reminded me of Margaret's family name—Lok and Locke, could they be the same? I filed this question away as I finished Wise's book.

Out of curiosity, I checked my Locke genealogical files to see whether this John Lok could have been one of Sir William's relatives. It seemed likely enough, given that Lok was a seafaring merchant from London, but my impression of Margaret's family had been that they were more involved in the Indian and Muscovy trade routes—silks, spices, and other luxury goods. I wasn't sure that this John Lok's cargo, as unusual as it was for London in 1555, had made much of a contribution to what was not yet a fully functioning transatlantic slave trade.

In my documentation on the Locke family, I found a pedigree chart that showed all descendants of Sir William Locke, colorful Sheriff of London. And turned out that John Lok was more than just a distant relative—he was one of Sir William Locke's sons. I then found that Margaret Locke Willoughby's great-grandfather Thomas, a half-brother of John, was an investor in that voyage to Africa, along with Sir George Barne, Sir John Yorke, Anthony Hickman (Thomas's brother-in-law), and Edward Castelin. The venture, as told by John Lok, is a catalog of fascinating direct observation and retelling of bizarre legends. Recognizable descriptions of the appearance, social behavior and habits of elephants are placed beside wide-eyed reports of wild men, "called Blemines, having their eyes and mouth in their breast" and "certaine Christians under the dominion of the great Emperour of Æthiopia, called Prester John." There is also a passage which sounds ominously like sales pitch: "There died of our men at this last voyage about twentie and foure, whereof many died at their returne into the clime of the colde regions, as betweene the Islands of Azores and England. They brought with them certaine blacke slaves, whereof some were tall and strong men, and could wel agree with our meates and drinkes. The colde and moyst aire doth somewhat offend them. Yet doubtlesse men that are borne in hot Regions may better abide colde, then men that are borne in colde Regions may abide heate, for-asmuch as vehement heate resolveth the radicall moysture of mens bodies, as colde constraineth and preserveth the same."5

That venture was hardly a blip on the screen of slavery history, and it was not immediately clear why the men had come along with Lok on his return journey. Lok himself described them as "blacke slaues", but as Sujata Iyengar points out, Lok's associate William Towerson "suggests that they were translators employed to enlist African support for the British against the Portuguese," who had already set up trading posts on the Ivory Coast. That said, Towerson was angrily questioned by a fellow Englishman when the captain admitted the Africans had been brought away from the coast "perforce," a word that means just what it says. They were to

---

5 Miranda Kaufmann, *Black Tudors: The Untold Story* (London: Oneworld Publications, 2017, 183), cites primary sources for both John Lok's 1554 voyage and that of his colleague William Towerson. Towerson landed in Ghana a year later to find the people questioning him about what had happened to the men taken away by Lok, who Towerson described in his account as having been removed from their village "perforce" or against their will.

be translators and be sent back home once their language skills were sufficient to assist English traders in breaking into the lucrative West Africa coastal trade. It was gold and ivory, adds Iyengar, that the English most prized, not human commodities. Yet just seven years after Lok brought his five Ghanaian men to London, John Hawkins made what is considered the true first step toward a transatlantic slave trade, an example which many were to follow, bringing wealth to slave traders and slave-owners and and untold misery for the next three hundred years to millions of enslaved human beings. And for those three centuries, I saw now—from the reign of Mary Tudor till the middle of the American Civil War—my enslaver ancestors were actors in that tragedy.[6]

During the CTTT conference call, I told this story—Eusebius' story, Thomas Lok's story, my story—to members listening on the other end of the line. I struggled to remain objective with a group of level-headed folk who I knew had already processed such history and the conflicted feelings it created. These men, after all, were dead. But it was not they who crowded my thoughts by day, my dreams at night. It was the people whose lives they had robbed, along with their bodies and their human dignity. Every few nights, people were screened in my dreaming mind so vividly I awoke feeling as if I had actually met them. The young black man called Randle, enslaved by my Lambright ancestors in Mississippi, who sat with me on a grass space near a white clapboard house, and started to tell me something but was prevented by a sharp shouting of his name from the porch. The elderly black woman wearing a turban, who approached my twenty-first century bed in her eighteenth century garments and struck the edge of the mattress with the flat of her hand, shouting at me, "You tell the truth! Tell it!" Perhaps, I wondered, rather than sharing these phenomena with the callers listening to me from all points of the globe, I should

---

[6] Iyengar, *Shades of Difference:*, 54.

consult a psychiatrist. Yet I realized my visceral response to events of the past, my determination to record the names of the people my ancestors enslaved, and even the dreams that troubled me at night, was welcomed by members of Coming to the Table. I would see a glimpse of this in a documentary produced and directed by Katrina Browne.

Traces of the Trade: A Story From the Deep North tracks the journey of ten white descendants of the DeWolf dynasty of slave-traders who not only explore the compass points of the Triangle Trade that made the DeWolf family of Bristol, Rhode Island rich, but following them also as each cousin makes an inward voyage into their family history and into consciousness of the impact their ancestors' slave trading had on thousands of human beings.

Thomas DeWolf's book about this journey, *Inheriting the Trade*, describes what it was like to stand for the first time in the deep mugginess of one of the basement holding pens to which his ancestors' slave cargo was consigned in Cape Coast Castle on the coast of Ghana. Crowded into the pen with his cousins and camera crew, DeWolf writes of what happened when the camera's battery pack fails, plunging the space into pitch darkness:

> I feel my way to a wall and sit on the rock floor. It doesn't matter if my eyes are open or not. The view remains the same. No one speaks. My thoughts drift in the silence.... I begin to put my-self in another time, another body.... I imagine be-ing here two hundred years ago with no lights, no comforts; only those three small holes far above connect me to the world outside this hard room and stifling heat.... I can only hear and feel and smell. What I hear and feel and smell are the worst

things I've ever sensed in my life. My heart beats
rapidly within my aching body.[7]

Tom, the others, black and white, begin to sob in the darkness, which two hundred years ago had been filled with far
many more people—black people—the floors slippery with
urine and feces. Through Tom's experience, I understood
those sobs, those terrors.

Now, though, talking over the telephone with Thomas, I
heard the kind, open voice of the type of guy you can lean
on in any emergency; the suffers-no-fools cadences and
flashing wit of Chicago-native Sharon Morgan, a descendant
of enslaved African Americans who would co-author a book
with Tom charting their voyage through their distinct and
intertwined family histories; the calm, measured music of
Susan Hutchison, who had long ago dealt with her peculiarly
American legacy of descent from a founding father who had
also fathered children on a slave. Susan had been part of an
effort to successfully petition the Monticello Association to
allow descendants of Thomas Jefferson and the enslaved
Sally Hemings to join the Association and have the same access to Monticello and its grounds, and to claim their Jeffer-
sonian heritage, as the third president's white descendants
were free to do. "What has to be faced, has to be faced," Susan would tell me later on. "And what has to be dealt with,
must be dealt with, in the fairest way, and in the heart's way."

Each voice on the line told me, based on hard-won experience, how liberating I would find it to be to simply tell the
truth of my family history. Part of telling that truth was to
do what Nina had asked me to do decades earlier—to find
descendants of the people our ancestors had held in slavery.
Yet I pointed out that this objective is easy to misconstrue.
Descendants of enslavers even looking for the descendants

---

[7] DeWolf, *Inheriting the Trade*, 104.

of their family's enslaved, as I had studied public records down till the trail went cold in the early 1900s, seemed to me to smack of white men hunting slaves escaped from a plantation. If the search affected me this way, how must it feel to the African American families I was reaching out to, from out of nowhere?

Given this, why on earth would descendants of people whom my forebears had enslaved want anything to do with me, especially if I came at them from out of nowhere, wanting who knew what from them—above all, reminding them of the im-balance of power that had once existed between my ancestors and theirs? This is where all my doubts about the whole enterprise had their genesis. Even as I sat in my kitchen beside the phone, they erupted and for a moment I wanted to hang up, forget what I had come for, put away the inventories and books about slavery and live the relatively normal life I'd known before this fierce angel challenged me to a wrestling match. But I couldn't stop reading the names. Moses. Vinia. Satin. Judy. Warren. Neptune. Juba. And Guy. And remembering something else my grandmother had said. This was about them, not about us. I had to know what had happened to them. Above all, I had to find, record and remember their names.

When Tom, Sharon, Susan and the others on the call heard that I had actually made contact with descendants of Guy Drock, and that the interest in doing so was reciprocated, I could feel an electricity crackle over the line. When I said I was hoping to meet Guy's descendants, I was urged to try to make it happen, provided the Drock descendants were in agreement. "I am planning to ask them if we can see each other in Norwich," I said. "It's where our shared history began."

One of those joining the conference call just then was an African American man named Joseph McGill.

Then a field officer for the National Trust for Historic Preservation as well as historical consultant for Magnolia Plantation and Gardens in South Carolina, Joe has a smoky, soft voice with a center of steel—even when he murmurs, he means business. When he introduced himself, he spoke more about his work than about who he was; as I was to discover, that's because his work *is* who he is. His work, indeed, had led him to embark on a historical experiment of his own, the Slave Dwelling Project.

In the course of his work interpreting at Magnolia Plantation, Joe had noticed the disproportionate interest in the main house over the extant slave dwelling at the back.

In the case of many plantation museums, people often arrive expecting to be wowed by "Tara", and often are, as docents sail them through high-ceilinged rooms with lace curtains and old Persian carpets, curving staircase banisters and elegant plaster-work. Provided someone thought to preserve one or more of them, however, out back are the cabins where slaves spent what free time they had to themselves, and these are often the least visited parts of such a property.

As Joe explained, when he tried to interest folks in the little cabin at Magnolia, they didn't seem to understand what the structure was for, or who had lived in it or, most significantly, how integral to all that made up the big house that cabin and its occupants had been. Dorothy Spruill Redford, whose journey back to her enslaved ancestors' pasts at Somerset Place in North Carolina, recalled being shown through the mansion by a guide who "mentioned the 'hired girls' who had kept house when the Collinses lived here. Those were her only two references," Redford added, "to the hundreds of my people who lived and worked here for almost a century." Then there were those who, far from denying slavery, seemed to want more evidence of it but for reasons different from Joe's.

At Magnolia, a visitor once asked why there was "only one" slave cabin out back—as if to say that surely more slaves were needed to keep this grand house in ship-shape, missing the tragedy at the core of what she said. "Ma'am," Joe responded, "it's one too many." He pointed out that without slaves, the big house could not have been built and run. Slave dwellings are usually very small, not distinguished by any architectural style or substance, he added, but they were the engine that kept the whole plantation viable. Yet these dwellings, built of substandard materials, were typically allowed to fall into ruins or razed to make way for the gardens of later residents of the main house, or removed because they made an inconvenient statement about the past. Joe noted that the tourist, who had been so garrulous before, now fell very silent.[8]

Starting with a few extant slave dwellings known to him, Joe had started spending the night in them, recording his experiences on his blog the following morning, in an effort to draw attention to the dwellings' existence and to appeal for help in restoring those few that were still standing. He had developed a mission statement, along with purpose, task and goal positions, that he shared with CTTT, hoping for our support in bringing "historians, students, faculty, writers, legislators, organizations, corporations, artists and the general public together to educate, collaborate and organize resources to save these important collectibles of our American history." He had thus far visited several sites within the South but was hoping one of us had information about a more northern slave dwelling. Because it was obvious to

---

[8] Note Margaret Biser's account of some of the reactions she had as an interpreter of plantations and slave dwellings in "I used to lead tours at a plantation. You won't believe the questions I got about slavery", http://www.vox.com/2015/6/29/8847385/what-i-learned-from-leading-tours-about-slavery-at-a-plantation; Redford, *Somerset Homecoming*, 99.

those who looked even a little bit under the carpet that slavery was not just a Southern institution.

That's when I remembered reading about a place I could hardly believe existed—Bush-Holley House in Greenwich, Connecticut.

Built starting in 1728 in what is now the suburb of Cos Cob, overlooking the harbor, by a Dutch farmer named Bosch (Bush), the two story house had remained in the family for over a century. In 1848, it was bought by the Holley family, in whose ownership it later became a boarding house popular with artists drawn to Cos Cob—names like Childe Hassam, Ernest Lawson, Theodore Robinson, John Henry Twachtman and J. Alden Weir spent time painting during summer stays there. Owned and operated as a museum by the Greenwich Historical Society, Bush-Holley House is a thriving destination for art lovers and history buffs both.

What made the house different from other historic homes in Connecticut is that along with the finely appointed rooms downstairs, it openly interpreted the slave quarters located over the kitchen wing at the back of the structure, quarters which had been the home of Candace Bush, the last enslaved woman to be freed in Greenwich and the only one whose grave boasts a headstone.[9]

I told Joe I knew of slave quarters in Connecticut. "None of the house's owners were related to me," I explained. "I've never been there. But the quarters look like they would work. It's just a matter of convincing the Greenwich Historical Society to agree to it."

---

[9] Mead, Jeffrey. "Chains Unbound: Slave Emancipations in Greenwich Connecticut Online": http://chainsunboundgreenwichct.blogspot.ca/2014/10/will-ye-even-sell-your-brethren-1995.html.

"Grant," said Joe, after a weighty pause. "If you can get them to let us in for a stay, would you care to join me?"

8 BLACK AND WHITE

The day of that conference call—September 24, 2011—I sent an email to Dr. Debra Mecky of the Greenwich Historical Society. I described my conversation with Joe McGill and told Dr. Mecky I had suggested that we approach her about setting up a Slave Dwelling Project stay in the Bush-Holley House quarters. "People find it incredible," I wrote to her, "that anyone north of the Mason-Dixon line owned other human beings." I hoped bringing SDP to Bush-Holley House would provide a rich teaching tool for the public, as well as mark a northernmost first for the Project. And then, I waited for a response.

As September rolled into October, I reached out to someone else—or, rather, to two others: Donald Roddy and Daryl D'Angelo, Guy Drock's descendants.

All my efforts to establish contact with descendants of people my ancestors had enslaved in the South had come to naught, and I was still saddened by this and unwilling to face the renewed possibility of another dead-end. Still, I was sure of one thing. Unlike the average folks on whose doors I, a strange white man, had come knocking unawares, an unknown and perhaps unwanted quantity, Don and Daryl were as passionate about seeking answers and following the chronological continuum to find them as I was. Our link was not at all hazy or based on a guess. My ancestor had owned theirs, had sold theirs, and remained in some sort of contact, through his descendants, with their ancestor's descendants. Then I had a response from Donald Roddy.

A former airline pilot living in Washington State, Don happened to be in Florida when he caught my email. He was pleasant, helpful. He told me he was happy to hear from me, and that when he returned home he would share more information. In the meantime, he had heard that Daryl was privy to results from a series of DNA tests done on male Drock descendants, with a view to discovering whether Benajah Bushnell's apparently kind treatment of Guy Drock had been partly occasioned because Benajah was the young man's father. Don had not been in touch with Daryl for some time, so was not sure where matters stood. He shared her email with me and offered to send a note to her explaining that we had been in touch.

My email to Daryl reads, in part, "My grandmother's Southern ancestors were enslavers, but I was dumbfounded to find that her Connecticut ancestors had been, too... I have come close to making contact with descendants of my Southern ancestors' black family but only when I got in touch with Don did I have the honor of making contact with a descendant of Guy Drock, and now I am in touch with you."[1]

A wife and mother, photographer and writer, Daryl lived in a small town in southern New Hampshire, and that was all I knew about her, aside from the fact that she was a descendant of Guy Drock and had spent years researching her Drock ancestry. I don't know what response I was expecting, but when it came next day, it arrived in a burst of cheer. "Thank you for writing!" she emailed. "It's gratifying to know that 15+ years of work has brought about something positive or enriching for someone else."

> Dumbfounded. Yes. An excellent word for such discoveries. I felt the same way myself as I researched my lines. Every step of the way required a deliberate opening of the mind and a willingness to challenge all I thought I knew or had been told.

---

[1] Author to Daryl d'Angelo, December 7, 2011.

When I contacted Don a week or so ago, he mentioned that he'd heard from a descendant of Benajah Bushnell, and of course the note(s) that went out yesterday afternoon meant that contact was imminent. Thus, I was totally unsurprised when your email came in last night... yet for some reason I'm finding it difficult to frame a response. Once more, this astonishing family calls upon me to suspend expectations and drop mental barriers. It never gets any easier somehow.

Meeting you is an experience I look forward to enormously... although the contemporary Drock descendants may not be what anyone is expecting. Hopefully, though, you are already aware of the journey this family took.[2]

"This astonishing family" resonated with me. I felt Daryl's words spoke directly to my experience thus far on my own genealogical and historical journey back through time. I had tried to suspend expectations, only to find that I had let go of hardly any when all came tumbling down. And I could scarcely blame Daryl for needing time to frame a response—I was relieved she had made one despite that hesitation. In fact, I was still not sure, when I asked myself plainly, why I was doing this. Why was I sending emails to strangers with whom I'd last shared remotely contiguous history over two centuries earlier? I remember waking up the morning after Daryl's response, which had thrilled me the night before, and thinking: What have I just done?

I was to discover that Daryl, too, had had a similar reaction, not just the next day but for many days afterward. That said, these initial few emails were the beginning of a rich cascade

---

[2] Daryl d'Angelo to author, December 8, 2011.

of them, interspersed with "Hi, how are you?" messages on Facebook which evolved into deep soul spelunking sessions.

Almost without variation, I was presented the problems that needed solving, while Daryl patiently picked apart my self-justifications for the emotions I readily brought to research and interpretations of what I found, constantly questioning what I came to see were my powerful prejudices against my own slave-owning forebears—people I had come to see as caricatures rather than complex human beings. They were not to be exculpated, Daryl said. But it was beneficial to my research and my state of mind to see them and their times as they were, particularly the ancestors who were enslavers in New England.

It was Daryl, ironically, who tutored me in the rigor of seeing Benajah Bushnell as a fully-fledged, multi-faceted personality—not the one-dimensional cardboard cut-out that my modern sense of justice, outraged by his complicity in slavery, had insisted he was.

She also encouraged me to take a deep look at what northern slavery was, as compared to Southern slavery—to see the picture from 180 degrees; to put my outrage aside, as they were not solving the problems my history posed to me; to stop judging the Bushnells and my other ancestors without considering the broader, richer picture of New England slavery, economic and social realities, and other factors of the period. In short, Daryl became my teacher in the art of looking back at and appreciating history without twisting it to suit my outrage over injustices committed in the past.

Some of our email and text discussions began innocuously, while some, like this one, began with a challenge—an approach Daryl specialized in.

Daryl: Tell me something (if I may ask) – are you angry with your ancestors?

Me: I don't know if it's possible to be angry at them and to avoid judging them, or the other way around, but that's sort of where I'm at.

Daryl: Sounds like it. Slavery was not a concept that was introduced to the world by North America. I think, particularly in New England and in colonial times, it was seen more as an historical norm that carried to the new world. It was the plantation approach – and particularly cotton – that fostered the terrible legacy we have to deal with today. I guess it's because I have no southern roots that I am not heated on the subject. Whatever it is, though, I don't feel particularly strong emotion when contemplating, say, my ancestor Guy's situation.

Me: I knew about the southern slavery before I ever suspected anything like it existed in the New England part, so I confess I come at that part of my history with the outrage I feel over what my more recent forebears did to people of color in the south.

Daryl: But is treating all your ancestral lines as equally guilty fair to them, do you think? Come out of the South with me. Picture instead the successful store owner in, say, Boston. He has built a strong business. Makes oodles of money. Nice house. Wife in lace. Girls with tutors and piano lessons. And, let's say, he has two "house servants". The servants in this scenario are more ornamental. They did not build that man's wealth as slaves did in the South.

Me: No, they didn't, but that he doesn't have to pay his enslaved housemaid or yardman means he is putting that pay into something else—building his business, buying his daughter a new dress—and that money is tainted because it is not going where it should, to the enslaved who rightly earned it.

Daryl: But saying the money isn't going where it should is to put today's moral lens on the subject. It's a wicked tangled mess. But Grant... it's not yours to atone for. You did not do it. The people who did it are dust. Yes, telling the stories is healing. The more the ignorance is dispelled, the more wide the understanding and hopefully acceptance of our shared past. But continuing to berate/blame – either direction –does not move us forward. Meaning, modern society.[3]

Daryl had lived in the South and with Southerners long enough, she said, to see the world from their side, or from the inside of their world, which was itself a separate state of reality. Because of this I had asked her advice about what to do when I visited a plantation museum in Georgia which had been built by slave labor. I admitted I wasn't sure I could do it; prior efforts to face this history had failed.

For example, when in Atlanta on a research trip, I had tried driving my rental car west to Troup County, where my great-great-great-grandfather John Kelly had been overseer on a plantation. I made it to the city limits of LaGrange, and a force that seemed uncontrollable even had I tried to reverse it made me pull over and turn the car around, back in the direction whence I'd come.

---

[3] Daryl d'Angelo to author, October 5, 2012.

Hearing about this, Daryl suggested to me that I actually had a rather Southern take on the history which both attracted and repelled me. "Only northerners (the winners, natch) hold the view that the Civil War is long ago," she told me. "I'm not trying to suggest in any way that your emotions are not valid. I am, however, suggesting that most of the folks I've encountered in the South take a longer view. You are much more recently come to this knowledge about your antecedents than I (much less Americans who find they have African ancestry). I was *far* less emotionally detached some years ago." She encouraged me to subdue my fears and visit that place built, worked on, lived in by slaves.

> When you visit that house, my friend, try to embrace more than the slavery-specific aspects. Reach for the feeling of time. Of age. The slave-holders are easy targets. But they are dead, Grant. Be irked in the cemetery. Maybe you'll think I'm weird, but I actually suspect that if Northerners didn't view all white Southerners as racist former plantation owners or all black Southerners as suffering former slaves, history might actually begin to recede.[4]

As if to underscore what she meant by this, Daryl sent me a link to a blog post she'd written in 2005.

> One frigid winter morning in Northern New York, my three-year-old asked,
>
> "Mommy, are we black?"
>
> I don't know how often this comes up in the average American household, but I'm guessing it's not often. Certainly it wasn't covered in the FAQs of my parenting books.

---

[4] Daryl d'Angelo to author, October 5, 2012.

I first found a black plastic spatula in the kitchen, and put it next to my hand, and then hers. "Are we this color?" I asked. The answer was no.

I then took us both outside, into the 2+ feet of new snow, and we rested both of our hands lightly on top. "Are we this color?" I asked. Again, the answer was no.

The world cannot be defined in such stark terms, and people who insist on doing so – no matter who they are – are either simplistically child-like, or have an agenda to promote.

My answer to her – and I believe this absolutely – is that we are all varying shades of beige. Did I complicate my child's life with this answer? Yes, I did – and we continue to discuss the issue still.

For many people, my daughter's question would have been a "no-brainer"; if you see the world in black and white, it's not a difficult concept. I, too, can see the world this way – but when I put those particular glasses on, my lenses show a social construct rather than a biologically determined outcome.

Frankly, black and white belongs in old photographs or artistic graphic design. I much prefer the vibrant hues of today. When you come right down to the bottom line, we are just people.[5]

Struggling with my own response to my personal history, with how to respond to these contacts I had made—as ineluctable, indeed, as the force which had drawn me out to

---

[5] "Mommy, Are We Black?" (posted October 2, 2005): http://www.polimom.com/2005/10/02/mommy-are-we-black/

the former plantation only to reverse course again—and what to do with them now that I had made them, I found myself leaning more and more on Daryl's wisdom, dispensed to me from her computer in snowbound New Hampshire to my sunny desk on the west coast, offering me the benefit of her warm good sense, and astonishing me continually with a generosity that I had never expected to experience from the descendant of a person my ancestors had held and worked as a slave.

Daryl told me I'd had a similar effect on her. "I think meeting you brought my entire ancestry out of the 'academic exercise' realm and made it all real," she said. To make it really real, however, we had to meet in person, she, Don and I.

The DNA tests to which Don had referred earlier at our first contact turned out to be disappointing to me, though even more interesting to Guy Drock's descendants: the male line back to Guy showed no influx of Caucasian DNA, which ruled out Benajah or any other white man as his father, but it did show that his origins were somewhere in Cameroon.

We didn't share blood, Daryl, Don and I. We shared a story far deeper.

9 OLD BONES

Not quite a month after I'd reached out to her, Dr. Debra Mecky of the Greenwich Historical Society reached back.

"I am very interested in your proposal," she wrote, "to bring the Slave Dwelling Project to Greenwich.... To my knowledge, Bush-Holley House is one of only two historic houses in Connecticut that have furnished spaces that interpret slave quarters.... I think the publicity and understanding that Joe McGill would bring to the topic of preserving the history of slavery in New England would make a significant contribution." We scheduled the panel discussion followed by the Slave Dwelling Project sleepover for March 30-31, 2012.[1]

For panel members, I already knew who I wanted—it was just a matter of gaining their interest and getting them there.

After talking with members of Coming to the Table, I knew we had to have writer Dionne Ford Kurtti and the Rev. David Pettee, both active CTTT members and speakers.

A descendant of enslaved and enslavers both, Dionne brought a family history to the table that beggared fiction. "Whenever I mention certain cousins," Kurtti wrote, "I have to put air quotes around the word so my husband knows which ones I mean. No air quotes means they're the ones I'm related to through blood. Air quotes, and I'm referring to the ones whose family used to own mine. They are my cousins through slavery." Kurtti descends from an enslaved woman named Tempy Burton who was inherited by Elizabeth McCauley, bride of Col. W. R. Stuart, a Louisiana cot-

---

[1] Debra Mecky to author, October 13, 2011.

ton broker. Tempy would bear children fathered by Stuart, who are captured in a group photograph of Col. and Mrs. Stuart sitting on the front porch of their house with Tempy in the middle and her two light-complexioned daughters on either side. "Tempy's expression is haunting, as if she's trying to solve a puzzle," explained Kurtti in a 2013 magazine essay. "The puzzle I need to solve: Why would she pose for what amounted to a family portrait, a good 25 years after slavery ended, with people who stole her freedom?"[2]

If Dionne brought a rare perspective from Southern enslavers and enslaved, Rev. Pettee's personal history outdid anything I had to share where New England slavery was concerned. In a handout written for CTTT, Rev. Pettee wrote, "Most of my ancestry is deeply rooted in New England and I grew up learning about Pilgrims, Puritans and minutemen. Not slavery." An amateur genealogist, the Unitarian Universalist minister would spend his free time exploring branches of his family tree, noting any new information that arose. Through Ancestry.com, Rev. Pettee found evidence of black people living in the home of an ancestor, Edward Simmons, in Newport, Rhode Island in the mid-1770s. Probing further, he discovered that Simmons owned the four African people listed in his household, and like me, he found that Simmons was not his only New England enslaver ancestor. In fact, he has located, to date, over forty more New England ancestors who owned slaves, and has met with descendants of one of them.[3]

---

[2] Kurtti, "My Family Tree: In Black & White" in *More: For Women of Style and Substance*, (August 7, 2013): http://comingtothetable.org/wp-content/uploads/2013/10/My-Family-Tree_-In-Black-and-White-_-MORE-Magazine.pdf.

[3] Pettee, "Ghosts of the Masters": https://ghostsofthemasters.wordpress.com/2011/05/14/a-case-study-in-researching-northern-slave-holding-ancestry/

After further discussions with Joe McGill and Dr. Mecky, it was determined that Dionne and Dave would join us in the Bush-Holley House quarters after the panel discussion.

Aside from Joe and me, I asked two more people if they would join us for the panel.

Dr. Allegra di Bonaventura, recently appointed Dean of Yale's Graduate School of Arts & Sciences, was working on a book which touched on my own family history—a history of the relationship between New London diarist Joshua Hempstead (1678-1758) and his enslaved African man, Adam Jackson. Hempstead was a jack of all trades, even inscribing pre-carved grave markers, and was the go-to guy for everything central to New London's business. He was also a friend and relative to Col. Jonathan Latimer, my seventh great-grandfather, who was mentioned in Hempstead's detailed records of daily events mundane, tragic and comic, and who, like him, also held a single African male (Caesar) in slavery in New London.[4]

What Allegra's research was exploring was how integral a presence Adam Jackson was in those diaries and in Hempstead's life. Jackson was a slave, yet also a partner in running the big show that was Hempstead's busy life; there was a closeness between the men akin to family members who've lived together many years—ultimately over forty in their case—yet Jackson slept in a spare attic space, unheated in winter and airless in summer. In the process of delving into this history, Allegra's work unfolded to offer an image of life in New London that took in not just the eccentric religious reformer John Rogers and the Rogerenes, the ups and downs of landed and feckless families like the Livingstons and Lechmeres, but also compassionately examined the least recognized of the town's lives, those of slaves and servants,

---

[4] Brown and Rose, *Black Roots in Southeastern Connecticut,* 473.

Indian and African, and how these bondsmen negotiated their way through a world in which their hopes for better were usually countered with worse.

The second person I hoped could join us was Dale Plummer, town historian of Norwich, whom I had met via email and telephone.

A descendant of Capt. John Mason, who was infamous for his role in the Pequot Wars, Dale was responsible for most of the research which had been done on Guy Drock the body of which had helped Don Roddy and Daryl D'Angelo join the remaining links together. Besides his work to identify and establish key sites and records pertaining to Norwich's black community, Dale was chairman of the Emancipation Proclamation Commemoration Committee, which would eventually unveil a Freedom Bell in Norwich's main plaza on the sesquicentennial of the Proclamation in 2013. On top of everything else Dale was doing, he was figuring out how to bring Daryl, Don and me together in Norwich on March 29, and how best to commemorate what he was certain was the first time in over two and a half centuries that a descendant of the Bushnells and descendants of Guy Drock had made a concerted effort to meet each other in the town on the Thames.

I had already fantasized for years what this first meeting with linked descendants would be like.

In that fantasy, I would drive down a long and winding Deep South road, frayed asphalt edged with the rough lace of rusted barbed wire, a few cattle or horses ruminating in warm golden fields, the summer snow of cotton dolloped atop brittle brown stalks, and I would find some piece of land where my ancestors had lived. There would be an unpretentious wooden house, where even shade trees did little to cool the bug-buzzing air. I would find there the descendants of people my people had enslaved, and we'd spend the day together in reunion. I would tell them, each one of them, that I was sorry for what my ancestors did to them, and somehow, though my apologies were embarrassing and indeed unnecessary against the expressions on their faces, in the pressure of their hands, they put up with me, much the way Daryl did when I poured out what she amusedly called my "endless liberal guilt". But of course, there was nothing I could say that the quiet, the falling sun, busy cicadas and a sky full of stars wouldn't say far better.

Given this absurd fantasy, with its overtones of stereotypes and paternalism only visible to me when I recorded it on a page, it may be imagined what it was like when I found myself on my way to actually meet descendants of someone enslaved by my ancestors. This time, I drove a winding road not in the Deep South but through the low wooded hills of southeastern Connecticut, to be exact—and not in Southern heat ebbing at twilight but through a silver-green spring day, too chilly to leave my jacket in the car when I arrived in Norwich, "the Rose of New England". And when I stepped out of my rental car, which I had parked in front of the austerely handsome red face of the Leffingwell House, almost as if in a dream, I had that surprise that comes with all awakenings: the woman and man who stood talking to Dale Plummer were white.

I should have guessed this might be the case, but for the stubborn persistence of preconception. I had seen a very small, indistinct photograph of Don Roddy on his Drock family history page. I could not tell from it what he really looked like save for the fact that he had a bushy white Santa Claus beard. I had never been able to locate a photo of Daryl, so imagination had eagerly filled the vacuum, overlaying black features where, I now saw, none were.

I remembered something Daryl had written me in her first email: "the contemporary Drock descendants may not be what anyone is expecting." She had clearly been preparing me for this moment, for which the term "cognitive dissonance" could have been specially invented.

Four white strangers embraced there in front of the Leffingwell House, but we didn't have much to say of consequence, at least at that moment. Daryl later told a reporter, "I don't have any of the cultural and social legacies of someone who grew up identified as an African-American, and I still had a moment of, 'What does this guy want from me.'"[5]

She was right to wonder—I didn't quite know myself what it was I wished for from this encounter.

Years later, Daryl would suggest to me that my almost proximity to my ancestors' lives and deeds—to the dead who, for me, were very much alive—might be a result of my being a writer, of having a mind that sees pictures along with words, puts breath back into dust long buried. (Indeed, her accurate comment recalls a line written by Ta-Nehisi Coates, whose mother had taught him, as my grandmother had taught me, "the craft of writing as the art of thinking."[6]) She also believed it was because of my grandmother's Southern heritage, which I had absorbed from her.

Just being in Norwich had reordered my coordinates, much the way my GPS recalculated every time I took a wrong turn from point A to point B. I had internalized the fact, known to me from books and from my own family's history, that

---

[5] Benson, "Descendants of Norwich slave, owner meet," *Norwich Bulletin*, March 30, 2012: http://www.norwichbulletin.com/article/20120330/NEWS/303309901

[6] Coates, *Between the World and Me*, 51.

slavery existed in New England, but when I looked at these people who were the progeny of one of my Norwich ancestor's slaves, yet visibly no different from anybody else wandering around the town at this early hour, it was as if that history were still being concealed from me, as if I were here on a fool's errand, duped by a treasure map leading nowhere.

That was about to change.

A Leffingwell House docent named Judith arrived to give us a tour of the house, which normally was still closed to the public at this time of year. I who had worked as a journalist and had never been afraid to ask questions found myself tongue-tied; Daryl, happily, had no such reservations. Looking up at the facade of the house, she asked Judith, "Are there still slave quarters in the attic? That's where they usually put them." Judith paused a moment, then shook her head. "The attic has been reconfigured so often since the old days, it's impossible to tell how it was originally arranged or used," she explained. She hesitated again, then added, "But I will tell you something. I live in a house that once belonged to the Huntington family. They were one of the families who owned many slaves. And I am quite sure I've found evidence in my attic that slaves were kept there."

She said no more. With that, we entered the cold, creaking Leffingwell mansion.

I'd visited castles in Germany and manor houses in England. But there is nothing like an old New England house. Many of them bear the same characteristics. They creak. They are cold. Yet there is something about an eighteenth century saltbox house that is like no other dwelling. Edith Wharton described it in her novel, *Summer*: "Inside... wind and weather had blanched everything to the same wan silvery tint; the house was as dry and pure as the interior of a long-empty shell."[7] There was a dry purity, the hardness and fragility of a conch shell, in these old dwellings which seemed to me peculiarly New England in character, not replicable anywhere else, and that same purity, toughness, gentleness seemed impregnated in the walls of the Leffing-well House. We passed through chill rooms that were blocks of winter immune to the spring unfolding outdoors, each full of gorgeous colonial paneling, age-blackened ceiling beams, wide plank floors that cracked like buckshot as crossed them. We paused to peer into glass cases displaying the sheen of old family silver, flintlock guns, Thomas Leff-ingwell's silver-topped walking stick. (Had Robin or Embar, I wondered, ever carried it for him? It was another question which, now that I was here, I dared not ask.)

But Daryl continued to ask all the questions I could not: When was the last time a Leffingwell descendant lived in the house and who was that person? Did any of the family keep in contact with former slaves? How many slaves, at most, did the Leffingwells own? Judith did her best to answer what I could tell were questions she had not expected and not in such rapid succession. Then we descended a narrow flight of steps and turned a corner into a daylight basement under the house, built into the lee of the hill on which the house sat.

It was even colder down here than upstairs; pale March morning light struggled to penetrate plastic sheeting over a couple of windows, next to which was a short, square door, very old, that appeared to be permanently sealed.

We stood there together for a moment. The atmosphere silenced even Daryl's questions. Then Dale said, "You know, that is the 'north door' you see over there. That is the door that Frances Caulkins referred to when she related the local

---

7 Wharton, *Summer*, 72.

tradition that slaves had been auctioned at the north door of the Leffingwell house."

That's when I finally opened my mouth. "So we're looking at Norwich's version of the 'door of no return'," I suggested.

Nobody spoke for a time. Standing there, I thought back to Tom DeWolf's experience of the lightless basement holding pen under Cape Coast Castle in Ghana, outside of which all that could be heard was the pounding of waves, as if echoing to the pounding of his heart. At the castle was a door leading out to the open sea, through which the enslaved were taken to be rowed to the waiting slave ship. "This is where slaves were kept before they were auctioned?" I asked.

"The house wasn't always here, you know," Judith told us. "It stood out near where you take the highway off ramp to Norwich. When the highway was being built, the house had to be moved. I have spoken with old timers who knew the house well, and had been all through it. They told me," she said, speaking low as if we were in church, "that there were shackles set into the stone walls in the basement." Looking around, Daryl said, "Where are they now?" The answer to that question was obvious. Judith shook her head. "When the house was moved, the basement itself was plowed over and flattened for the highway," she said. "Whatever was down there was buried by the demolition work."

Burial seemed the order of the day, the theme of our reunion.

Dale guided Daryl, Don and me to Norwichtown's cemetery, where several of my ancestors had their graves marked out by thin, illegible stones, each with the tilted angle of very old people trying to find equilibrium. But equilibrium had long ago been lost, I saw, to the black people buried at the bottom of the hill. There I found the stone of Boston Trow Trow, locally famous African "governor", whose rank had not earned him interment at the top, among the Bushnells and Leffingwells, Arnolds and Huntingtons. Yet his funeral was likely a much more dramatic memorial than those of the sober white Puritans above. "Dressed in their best finery, accompanied by music and song, black men and women generally marched en masse to the burial ground," writes Ira Berlin. "Evoking practices of African memory," these mourners would have placed ornaments of special meaning upon the corpse and its grave. And the burial spot would not be bereft after the ceremonies were over; African slaves were known to return with food and rum to leave for their departed loved ones, while watched from afar by suspicious or scornful white people as "the Heathenish rites are performed at the grave by their countrymen."[8]

I signaled the others to join me, and we tried to stand there on the steep incline, looking down at the stones and, beyond, to a parking lot with a lone dumpster standing at an angle, like someone with a weight on their conscience who cannot bear to look anywhere but away.

Gravestones and bones greeted us again: we were next taken into the low-ceilinged basement of the Victorian stone building which was the successor to the church for which Benajah Bushnell had donated the land.

There, in gloom made muggy by a chugging furnace, we found the gravestone of my eighth great-grandmother Zerviah Leffingwell Bushnell, its crest topped with a chubby smiling cherub's face between two softly feathered wings. "But why are all these stones stacked under the church?" I asked. Dale explained, "When the property was developed down the line, the graves had to be moved. The stones were

---

[8] Berlin, *Many Thousands Gone:*, 62.

all brought to the basement for safekeeping." "And the bones?" I asked.

"Come with me," Dale said.

Upstairs, we walked down the aisle of the church, Daryl, Don, Dale and I. The high Gothic Revival windows bathed the shadowed interior in pale rainbows. "The bones are all under here," Dale told us, stepping up to the altar. "Where was Guy buried?" I asked Daryl. "He died in Preston," she replied. "Could he have been brought back to Norwich for burial?" I pursued. "And wouldn't it have made sense for him to be buried near the church where he was baptized?" "Perhaps," Daryl murmured cautiously. "But does it matter? Bones are bones."

We stood there quietly, over all those bones—Benajah's, Zerviah's, possibly Guy's, all mixed together, perhaps, slave and free, indistinguishable.

From the hush of the church, we walked with Dale through the echoing halls of Norwich Free Academy, a school founded in 1856 by Norwich minister John P. Gulliver.

Daryl, Don and I took seats at three desks lined up in front of the United States history class of teacher Karen Cook, who had devised a bold lesson plan. All eyes were upon us, including those of Leo Butler, Director of Diversity for the Academy and a descendant of slaves from Mississippi—a sea of white students' faces from which one face of color stood out conspicuously.

Karen explained what was about to happen. "We are honored to have with us today three people who have met here in Norwich for the first time," Karen told the class. "One of them is descended from a slave owner, Benajah Bushnell, who lived in Norwich in the eighteenth century. Two of them are descended from the African slave owned by Bush-nell. Let's take a vote on who had the slave ancestor and who the slave-owner."

Karen said, "OK, now let's hear who you think, first, is descended from the slave Guy Drock." There was little hesitation. I was pointed to unanimously. I turned to look at Daryl, who was correctly fingered as a Drock descendant, and she winked at me.

"And... who is descended from Benajah Bushnell?" asked Karen. Everyone agreed that had to be Don, whose white beard made him look patriarchal, I had to admit—perhaps similar to an enslaver of the South, but nothing like spectacled and likely clean shaven Benajah Sr. of eighteenth century Norwich.

"Then you're in for a surprise," said Karen. "These two—Daryl and Don—are Guy Drock's descendants. Grant is descended from Benajah Bushnell."

There was general astonishment; eyes turned to me, then avoided me.

We were asked to speak to the class about what had led us to where we were that day.

Don talked about how the paperwork attached to a Civil War pension application had taken him back through time, to other documentation that introduced him to an ancestor he had never heard of, a heritage he could not have imagined. "I had no idea I had African ancestors until a few years ago," Don explained. "No one in my living family had a clue about that."[9]

I told my story, starting with the fact that my Southern slave-owning history would never have led me to believe in my wildest dreams that I would be sitting in a school in Norwich, Connecticut, talking about my New England slave-owning ancestors with two descendants of one of their slaves beside me.

Then Daryl spoke.

"I liked you as a person, right away," she said, looking at me. Turning back to the class, she added, "But the initial contact was really weird."

> I had all sorts of reservations about this because....
> Well, look. It took me a *decade* to get to a place
> where I could see all of who I am. For years, for
> most of my life, I thought I was Native American,
> that my great-great-grandfather had been a scout
> for Lafayette, because that was the story my family
> told. Getting from there to the Drock house and
> Dale Plummer in Norwich, Connecticut has been a
> long journey. And at every stage of that I learned
> about myself. I learned I had preconceptions. Be-
> ing Indian was already a stigmatized designation,
> but being black was worse. My family chose to
> identify with the lesser of the two risks. I have had
> to look inside myself and figure out why I could

---

[9] Benson, "Descendants of Norwich slave, owner meet," *Norwich Bulletin*, March 30, 2012: http://www.norwichbulletin.com/article/
20120330/NEWS/303309901. In 2015, Dale Plummer organized a
group visit from several Drock descendants to christen a paver in Norwich's David Ruggles Freedom Plaza. The paver was laid 256 years to
the day when Sarah Powers purchased Guy's freedom from Benajah
Bushnell.

not accept that I have two images in my face, there to see every single day. So when Grant contacted me, I didn't know what to think, because I was still trying to get used to it all myself. Now, though, I'm really glad you did.[10]

Leo Butler, Norwich Free Academy's diversity director, had come to audit the class after hearing about our visit from Karen. Visibly moved, he thanked us afterward, stating that not only had the session made him think differently about the work he does at the school, but also about research he's done on his own family, with origins in Southern slavery.

"A lot of what you're talking about is difficult in some ways for me to hear," Leo told us. "My great-grandfather was born in Mississippi as a slave." He added that our effort to reach out to each other, descendants of enslaved to descendant of enslaver, had moved him to do something similar with white cousins from his mother's side of the family. "I know where they live," he smiled. "One of these days I'm going to go ring their doorbell."[11]

That broke the tension. We laughed, but I wasn't the only person in that classroom who wondered what kind of response Leo might receive when and if that door opened.

---

[10] "Descendants of slaves and slave owner visit Norwich", video: John Shishmanian; published March 29, 2012: https://www.youtube.com/watch?v=MSME0vRIei4

[11] "Descendants of slaves and slave owner visit Norwich", video: John Shishmanian; published March 29, 2012: https://www.youtube.com/watch?v=MSME0vRIei4.

I arrived in Old Saybrook from Norwich that afternoon, pulling up to the white Victorian house that was home to my friends Torrance and Patricia Downes and their golden lab, Zack.

After I'd stowed my bag at the top of pale-painted stairs washed in light from a stained glass landing window, Torrance, a board member of the Old Saybrook Historical Society, and I headed for the cemetery.

Cypress Cemetery is reckoned to be in its fourth century of use, but the oldest extant grave marker dates from December 1686. The marker memorializes a baby, Susanna Lynde, daughter of Nathaniel and Susanna Willoughby Lynde, my ninth great-grandparents. The infant died aged four months old.[1]

Susanna is not the only child in the Lynde plot. Her brother Willoughby, born ten years later, lived to be only seven, and is memorialized with a foot stone placed very close to a larger, later stone—evidently there was some rearrangement to make room for other members of the family over the course of time.

The dominant graves, of course, are those of Nathaniel and Susannah.

Against a backdrop of bright green grass made the more vivid by slanting afternoon sun, the Lyndes' red sandstone tablet monuments stood out with all the thrust of memorial

---

[1] Downes, "The Lyndes of London and Saybrook, via Boston": http://www.cypresscemeteryosct.org/lynde.html.

stonework I had seen in European churches, the only major difference being in their sylvan setting, away from church rafters, with just branches between their face and the sky. In fact this natural foundation has done wonderfully weird things to markers meant by design to point straight toward the heavens. Nearly every Lynde gravestone had been thrown off the perpendicular by the encroaching roots of an enormous tulip tree, planted in the plot, near little Susanna's stone marker. This gave the family plot, and those who, like me, were unfamiliar with its drunken tilt, a strange sense of being off kilter, especially as behind the graves lay the flat silver expanse of South Cove, the Connecticut River, and the Atlantic Ocean—water that seemed more solid than earth.

The winds off that water were biting, the sun intermittent. But when Torrance asked me if I'd like to stay a while on my own, I told him I'd see him in an hour. It was worth spending time in this chill, for there was a fair bit of history here to absorb. "You may find the slave portion of the cemetery of interest," he added. Slave portion? I asked. "Yes," he said, "not that far from the Lyndes, actually. See those white stones over there? That's Rose Jackson, Phillis Jackson— they were sisters—and a male slave named Frank Ransome."

Torrance gave me a brief history of the Jackson sisters.

Rose was born in November 1778 in the family of General William Hart, and died in the family of Gen. Hart's son, Richard Hart, on October 18, 1866, having lived from the time of the War of Independence past the Civil War—an astonishing stretch of American history to have witnessed and experienced. As we stood in front of the three stones— Frank's smaller and rounded at the top, Phillis's broken and mended, and Rose's tall, sharply rectangular, and unblemished—Torrance explained that Rose was born into Gen. William Hart's household (if not purchased for it as an infant; it was believed to be best for a slave to be raised within her white family rather than brought in later as an adult[2]) but it is believed that Richard Hart actually owned her. Though technically freed in 1849, Rose refused to leave her white family, and continued to occupy her room over the kitchen.

"We know that Phillis was owned by another member of the Hart family," he said, "because when Phillis lay dying, Rose asked for permission to stay with her in her room at the Hart mansion." The following morning, Rose came downstairs, and on seeing her Mrs. Hart asked if Phillis had passed a good night. Rose told Mrs. Hart that Phillis had actually died late in the evening, around nine o'clock. Not wanting to wake up the Hart household, Rose had slept beside her sister's lifeless body till her white family had arisen for the day.

Torrance pointed out an anomaly in the orientation of the three slaves' gravestones. "All the older interments in this cemetery have stones with the engraved side looking to the north," Torrance explained, meaning the bodies themselves were buried with feet pointing south. He told me that the three markers for Frank, Phillis and Rose all have their engraved sides facing south, yet foot stones pointing north, which seems to indicate that they were deliberately buried per some different orientation. There was no way to tell, he added, whether the bodies were actually in that direction without exhuming them.

Given that Christian burial practice seemed more often than not to dictate an east-west orientation—the more convenient for facing both the rising sun and the last coming of Christ—all the Cypress Cemetery burials, which don't all face in the approved quadrant, would seem problematic. Yet what struck me was that Rose was not buried with her white family, the only people she had ever known. Yet this is what they had carved on her stone:

In memory of Rose Jackson
Born 26 November 1778, Died 18 October 1866
A colored woman who for nearly seventy years
was trusted and faithful servant in the family of
Gen. William Hart and of his descendants to the
fifth generation.
Faithful Ever In All Things[2]

Torrance left me then, as he had some errands to run. "Just wander at will," he smiled. I tried to. I had meant to check out the Yale Boulder, a marker placed to commemorate the 1701 founding of what later became Yale on property Nathaniel Lynde had donated for the use of the Saybrook Collegiate School. I also had on my list the gravestone of Lady Alice Fenwick, a sandstone monument said to have been carved by my ancestor Matthew Griswold. But I couldn't leave Rose Jackson's grave. Despite the cold winds off the water, the white marble seemed to radiate the warmth of stone having stood a long time in hot sun.

"The relationship which developed between the master's family and the slave cannot be overlooked as one of casual acquaintance," writes Donald E. Perrault. "In many instances this bond was stronger than that between other members of the same family." Not everybody understood this. Sarah Kemble Knight, the Boston-born diarist who died in Norwich in 1727, pronounced herself revolted by how familiar relations were between blacks and whites in rural New England, noting that in Connecticut slaves and masters sat at the same table together, "and into the dish goes the black hoof as freely as the white hand." Clearly, this closeness was not entirely as Miss Knight insisted, "as they say to save time" by eliminating separate arrangements.[3]

---

[2] See cypresscemeteryosct.org/113-2/

[3] Perreault (citing Piersen), "Forgotten Voices," 57-59

Citing William D. Piersen's *Black Yankees,* Perrault mentions the recorded last wishes of two New England slaves named Ginney and Aaron. Ginney had come from Africa and been enslaved by the Rev. William Worthington of Saybrook. On her deathbed, speaking to a reverend, "she was said to have described her vision of paradise to be much like her former life in Saybrook: 'Yes, Massa Goodrich,' said Ginney, 'when I die I shall go to heaven, and knock at de door, and inquire for Massa Worthington.... Massa Worthington will come right to me; and I will say, 'Ginney's come. I want you to tell God that Ginney was always good servant. She never lie, never steal, never use bad language.' And then he will come back to the door and say, 'Ginney, you may come in.' And I will go right in, and sit in the kitchen.'" Aaron belonged to the Morton family of Massachusetts. When near death, the elderly slave was heard to ask that he might be buried close to the family home, the better to "hear de chilluns' voices when dey be playing."[4]

Perhaps that was what most moved me about Rose Jackson. She had mothered five generations of Hart family members—indeed, she had likely been put to work in the Hart household before she had had a chance to know what it was like to be fully mothered herself. As surrogate mother across a racial divide, Rose had held a certain authority, and can be imagined being asked for counsel as well as comfort by members of the Hart family. Yet it is clear that even into her eighties, she was treated more like a child than an adult, because whatever her gifts of mothering, she remained an African woman, a servant, of a race listed in inventories just above the livestock, and as incapable of making decisions as a horse or cow. And like the black slaves of Norwichtown Cemetery, here in Old Saybrook Rose had been buried among other enslaved dead, far from the family she had served with body and soul.

---

[4] *Ibid.,* 57-58.

Born in 1908 in Old Saybrook's small African American community, author Ann Petry wrote not just of the racial discrimination she endured in the town but also of her anger on behalf of Rose Jackson. "Sister Rose", wrote Petry, by being buried facing the opposite direction from the Harts, and in a separate, less desirable portion of the burial ground, had been treated to "the 19th century equivalent of the back of the bus."

> Every time I have ever looked at [Rose's grave] I think about that spiritual, "On that great gittin' up mornin' I'll be there." Well, come the Day of Judgment, I am sure that Sister Rose Jackson will be there with all the other risen souls but Sister Rose Jackson, a colored woman, will be standing alone and she will be facing the swamp. The other folk will be facing the Main Street of the town.[5]

I placed my hands on the marble stone, which even here in a constant chill sea breeze held on to the warmth of the sun, not hot but the soft warmth of freshly baked bread cooling on a kitchen table. I looked out to that sea that was to be Rose Jackson's first view, if you believe in a day of resurrection. And I had a very hard time believing that Rose, whatever the insult we impute to her burial arrangements, would not take one look at Long Island Sound on the day of judgment, straighten her apron and turban, and turn, with her sister Phillis, to go find her white family, and walk with them wherever they were going, even if she specially deserved a heaven their eligibility for which might be considered to stand in some doubt. "Faithful ever in all things", would Rose Jackson have had it any other way?

---

5 Petry, *At Home Inside*, 31.

11 LIBATION

When you first see Bush-Holley House from the highway, particularly while driving south on the 95 as I was doing, you do a double-take.

The gracious two story structure, with its front verandahs and hint of square-shouldered Georgian dignity, sitting on the edge of a slope that drops down to Greenwich Cove, intersects jarringly with the impersonal concrete curve of the highway that rises on pylons practically beside it. From up here, surrounded by New York-bound traffic, the house seemed small, fragile, capable of disappearing like a bubble if pressed too hard.

That sense of being amazingly unreal continued. I was greeted by Debra Mecky, a warm, quietly smiling woman. Debra sent me off with staff member Zoe to give me a tour of the mansion.

As a former art critic, I was intrigued to see this residence which from the 1890s to the 1920s had been the epicenter of Impressionist painting in the state of Connecticut. Primary among the artists associated with the Cos Cob art colony, and thus with Bush-Holley House, were Childe Hassam, Canadian-American Ernest Lawson, Theodore Robinson, John Henry Twachtman and J. Alden Weir. Hassam had always been a special favorite of mine, which made encountering one of his watercolors in the front hall of the mansion a particularly pleasant surprise. Of the others, I knew that Weir had been one of the most popular practitioners of American Impressionism, an artist whose frank, generous style was matched by his open, generous heart. I was fascinated to see work by Yeto Genjiro [1867-192], who had started out a master potter in Japan and ended up an employee of the Japanese postal system, but in between had had a huge influence on the work of the Cos Cob art colony and a role in spreading awareness and appreciation of Japanese art and customs in America. Along with these treasures were those of a more mundane type—rooms filled with Persian carpets, silver displayed in antique sideboards, all the attractive Victorian clutter of a well-to-do middle class home interspersed with the noble profiles of colonial-era chests and chairs.

"Now let me show you the slave quarters," Zoe said. I followed her past the Hassam and up the stairs.

I don't know what I was expecting, but it was not this little door off the upstairs landing, or the sudden shift from painted paneling outside to rough plank floors and rafters within. I saw a long space, high in the middle in the roof's peak and cramped and dark at the edges. Through the floorboards I could see slivers of light from the kitchen below. Because this space would also have been utilized for storage purposes, there were boxes and trunks that one would have found in any New England attic, beside which were pallets with blankets and pillows where the Bush family's several slaves—Candice, Patience, Jack and Cull, along with others—would have slept. "It was originally much more cramped in here," explained Zoe. Post-slavery, alterations were made within the space to increase standing room and add windows.

So back in the time of Candice Bush, a woman would have had to bend or crouch, and squint, in this space, where there was considerably less space and less light than what I saw today. Despite that darkness, here may be where art and slavery intersected long before Hassam and Yeto graced the house's rooftree. Candice Bush had a daughter, Hester, who married a slave who had belonged to the prominent Mead family of Greenwich. The white Meads lived in a stately colonial house with several towering red brick fireplaces and a white picket fence. The Meads preserve to this day a watercolor of the house, painted on woven paper in the naive two-dimensional style of a sampler sometime between 1840-60 by a black woman who had worked for the Meads at that time. Though the painting is unsigned, the Mead family has good reason to believe Hester was the artist. Like the doll's house that was becoming so popular in that era as teaching tool for little girls to grow to womanhood knowing how to manage every detail of their circumscribed domestic world, perhaps the enslaved Hester painted that world the better to comprehend it, to own it, by returning its depiction from black hands to white ones.[1]

Amid this welter of impressions, there was not much time to contemplate where I would be spending the night.

Shortly, Joe McGill, a stocky man just into his fifties, arrived at the house. I had watched a couple of his video blogs posted to the Slave Dwelling Project's web site, so felt I knew what he was like. I just wasn't prepared for his profound, wordless self-sufficiency. With his bald head and warmly observant eyes, Joe reminded me of Buddhist monks I have known, men both anchored to the basic energies of this world and yet not at all of it, dwelling in their own perfect universe.

Yet for a man so in touch with the past and so aware of its value to the present, Joe was remarkably level-headed, even stubborn, and in large part this proceeded from a deep need to protect himself. I asked him if he had ever sensed the spirits of those who had lived in the thirty slave dwellings he had spent nights in thus far. He shook his head. "No, I don't want to go there," he told me, smiling but in no way com-

---

[1] Mead, Jeffrey. "Hester Mead: An Uncommon Artist?": http://mead-buryinggrounds.blogspot.ca/2009/10/hester-bush-mead-uncommon-artist.html

fortable with the topic. "Some people pick up on this stuff, and that's okay. Even if I could pick up on it, would I want to? No. Because my sense is that it would involve a lot of anger. And I have enough to do to control my own anger at the institution of slavery. I don't need ghosts egging me on with theirs."

Joe and I gobbled down a quick dinner, and then I saw Don Roddy walk into the Barn, an event space on the Bush-Holley House property where the panel discussion would be held. I hurried down to greet him. As we talked, more people filed in, including Joe, Dionne Ford Kurtti, Dave Pettee and Dale Plummer, followed by statuesque and smiling Dr. Allegra di Bonaventura, only a tad flustered by a traffic jam on the 95.

Jaime Villaneda, education director of the Greenwich Historical Society, arrived and we sorted out who would do what during the discussion.

I was the last to be seated at the panelists' table, between Dionne and Dave, with Joe closest to the podium. As Jaime described the evening's program and introduced each of us to the crowd, I noticed movement at the back of the hall. The people who were still coming in, and having to stand when they did, were almost uniformly black people. I thought again of the meeting-house scene in *The Witch of Blackbird Pond*. "The Puritan service seemed to [Kit] as plain and unlovely as the bare board walls of the Meeting house," wrote Elizabeth George Speare. "Kit's gaze flicked over the other churchfolk. A varied lot they were... and there, in the furthermost pews, Kit glimpsed the familiar black faces that must be slaves. All of them however were alike in their reverent silence."[2]

---

[2] Speare, *The Witch of Blackbird Pond*, 53.

Here, again, was a kind of New England meeting-house, and though two African American people were seated on the panel, and it was the year 2012, the "familiar black faces" were mostly in that familiar, unsettling place, at the rear of the room.

Joe began, "My purpose for being here today is that after you guys have gone your separate ways, and to a nice comfortable bed, I'll be spending the night here in the former slave dwelling at Bush-Holley House. Tonight will be my thirty-first stay in my ninth state. And tonight, for the first time, I will knowingly share the experience with a descendant of slave-owners. That in itself makes it quite interesting."

> What I'm finding out through this project is the role that slavery played on the American landscape. I've gone as far west as Texas, where I learned about cotton; to Missouri, where I learned about hemp farmed by slave labor. Tobacco in Maryland, sugar cane in Louisiana, where the profits were so big they could afford to work their slaves to death and just replace them rather than ensure they had appropriate food and shelter. And rice in South Carolina.
>
> The slaves who worked the rice fields had been brought deliberately from regions of Africa where rice was cultivated. In all these cases, there was agricultural experience and/or tradition that these enslaved people carried with them to America. Yes, slavery was about unpaid labor, and it was about brute force brought to bear on defenseless people. But these people brought with them many talents—not least a talent for survival of the worst mankind can throw at mankind. And it's vitally

important to preserve the places that sheltered them.[3]

Dave Pettee was next to hold the microphone. "Both sides of my family were colonizers of Massachusetts, Connecticut and Rhode Island, and I grew up with all those great stories of the past, along with the moral superiority of the north in terms of fighting the Civil War to end slavery," he explained. "I grew up with this clear idea of the sort of people I came from." Then he discovered, by accident that his Rhode Island ancestor, Edward Simmons, owned four African slaves. "I went to the archives to correct what I thought was a mistake," he said, "as there were no slaves in New England—*everybody* knew that—and while I was there I proceeded to find eleven other ancestral families in Rhode Island alone who were slave-holders. To make a long story short, I have found forty-two ancestors only in New England who owned slaves."

Once you become aware of a story like this within your family, most people try to push it away, or they find they need time to try and make sense of what it means to carry this type of history.

Coming to the Table as an approach has four features that feed one into the other—willingness to dig into the history of family or community and to be willing to take on the journey into the role slavery played in personal or public history; to help us try to make sense of this information we are finding which is so incredibly difficult to manage alone, and to help build community, which Coming to the Table has truly become.

---

[3] Transcribed from author's notes at event as well as from "Slaves in the Attic – Panel Discussion", Sound Bites from Panel Discussion, Friday, March 30, 2012. Greenwich Historical Society.

It's a community in which to find healing through various ways, whether through ritual or ceremony or reunions between linked descendants. Reaching out to each other in honest dialogue, creating a different kind of legacy to replace that in which African American and white folks have been driven apart by slavery and to work on current issues around racism that plague our communities today.[4]

As Dave spoke, I noticed that Dionne, sitting beside me, was wearing a vintage sepia photograph pinned around her neck. An elderly white couple occupied two chairs on a porch while in front of them, on the steps, sat a black woman flanked by two light-complexioned daughters.

I realized this was the image which had started Dionne on her quest, not dissimilar to Daryl's and Don's, yet even more complicated. Dionne identified as black, she told the audience, but when she asked her light-complexioned grandfather about his background—"Are you black?"—he refused to say. But he did tell her about his grandfather, Col. Stuart, the father of the two light-complexioned young women sitting on each side of their mother, Stuart's former slave, Tempy Burton. "When my enslaved ancestor was manumitted," Dionne explained, "she stayed, the rest of her life, probably because they were family."

> Look at my grandfather. He looked like my husband. But he called himself black because where he grew up if you called yourself white, you might not have made it to the next day—the one drop rule. It's hard when people ask you a question about "What are you?"

---

[4] Transcribed from author's notes at event as well as from "Slaves in the Attic – Panel Discussion", Sound Bites from Panel Discussion, Friday, March 30, 2012. Greenwich Historical Society

The concept of black and white is too small to encompass what we're talking about here. I also believe it's a construct that was *devised*. When I look at my ancestors—I'm from tribes. I'm from the Celtic tribe, I'm from various African tribes. I've gotten to the point where race doesn't do it for me. I say, "I'm a descendant of various Celtic and African tribes."

That may not do it for other people, but that's a better picture of it, for me, than saying I'm black.[5]

From the Deep South, Allegra veered us North to the simpler yet even more complex relationships of white enslavers and black enslaved as exemplified in the lives of Joshua Hempstead and Adam Jackson in New London. The interpenetration of slavery in all aspects of colonial New England life and the ironies each of those aspects reflected back at the others is summed up in a passage in her book, *For Adam's Sake: A Family Saga in Colonial New England*:

The small world of the early New England town was an interwoven and knotted mesh of individual and families that implicated every inhabitant. This social fabric held deeply ingrained patterns, but it also contained surprising patches of ambiguity and opportunity.... A slave might free himself from bondage, while his master, a son of privilege, crumbled and broke under the weight of his own pedigree.

A "mulatto" servant might imagine and even make himself "English", as his slaveholding neighbors signed their own sons over to years of

---

[5] Transcribed from author's notes at event as well as from "Slaves in the Attic – Panel Discussion", Sound Bites from Panel Discussion, Friday, March 30, 2012. Greenwich Historical Society

servitude. A kindhearted widower could devote himself to motherless children but still enslave another man's boy without a whiff of remorse.[6]

Dale Plummer was next. He spoke to his research into the life of Guy Drock and how first Daryl, then Don, and finally I had contacted him over a series of decades, culminating in yesterday's meeting in Norwich. He also brought the audience back to the New London area, having discovered through talking to Dave Pettee that they both shared descent from Capt. John Mason, founder of Norwich and leader of Connecticut colonial forces in the horrific Pequot War of 1636-37—"probably unequalled in savagery," he said, his voice halting with emotion, "to anything you have ever read about."

> The Pequot war was really one of the very first conflicts between settlers and Indians. It resulted in the enslavement of many of the Pequots—the victors exchanged Pequots for African slaves from the West Indies. The land on which most of southeastern Connecticut is built was never paid for. It was in fact taken from the Pequots. And few remember one of the worst episodes of the war.

> Pequot captives were gathered in summer 1637 by English soldiers in what they called New London, trussed up, taken out into the middle of the Thames River, and drowned. This hugely impacts the history of southeastern Connecticut, with the wealth that was amassed, with the whole question of race, social class, and so on for our area of New England.

---

[6] Bonaventura, *For Adam's Sake*, xvii.

Dale noted that he had met that morning with leaders from the Mashantucket Pequot Nation, he said, and realized as they spoke that his ancestral connection to their oppression was "something I have never really faced. This is why I'm so glad to meet members of Coming to the Table," he said, visibly moved. "Because I don't think the Pequots need *our* help—I think we need *theirs*."[7]

Suddenly, all eyes were on me, as well they might be.

After all, as they all knew from our introductions, I had ancestors complicit in every facet of experience shared by my fellow panel members—slaves North and South, African American relatives descended from white on black sexual exploitation, eviction and extermination of native peoples, selling, buying and working of slaves.

I began to speak to the history of the black people at the back of the room, to Don Roddy, whose African ancestor my white ancestor had owned, to the many white faces, from some of which this evening's information seemed to rebound back at us while others had absorbed it, troubled by the revelations it aroused. And as I spoke, I felt increasingly my old reservations: that while what we were doing here was worthy of everyone's time, it was not making a difference. People had brought prejudices and pocket personal histories along with them, and like any human being, many were unwilling to part with them even in the face of evidence to do otherwise.

This was especially obvious during the question and answer session that followed.

------

[7] Transcribed from author's notes at event as well as from "Slaves in the Attic – Panel Discussion", Sound Bites from Panel Discussion, Friday, March 30, 2012. Greenwich Historical Society.

One Greenwich resident, an older white man redolent of comfortable circumstances and certitudes, proudly recalled an exhibit in the city some years back of manumission documents. "The Greenwich archives are *filled* with these manumissions," he said, as if these pieces of paper wiped away two centuries of slavery in New England or made its lasting ramifications bearable for the people the documents freed. Indeed, many of their descendants may have been standing quietly at the back of the room.

Allegra asked the man what he made of the fact that freeing one's slaves had become as fashionable in the late eighteenth and early nineteenth centuries as the latest carriage design or style of drinking tea? Was that the same as coming to the conclusion that enslaving a human being was wrong and that freeing them was the right thing to do? Or was it more akin to one-upping the Joneses?

And what, I added, of slaves whose manumissions were conditional. Not just that of Guy Drock who, after all, was not freed but merely sold to the woman who wanted to marry him, but of Romeo, freed by his Leffingwell master on promise of continued service at the beck and call of the family for the rest of his life. "That is not freedom," I said.

The questioner was probably the only person in the room who was visibly digging in his heels on this topic, but to me it seemed as if every white person there was looking at me as if I were a traitor to my skin color. As I contended with this irritating impression, the faces of the black people standing at the back seemed almost universally creased with concern. "How far will he go with this?" they seemed to ask. "And why?" They echoed my own thoughts.

After that, it was over, and as people filed out, we panelists were photographed in a smiling row by the local press. Then the four of us crossed from the barn under a sky of dark, low-hanging clouds to Bush-Holley House. And Dionne, Joe, Dave and I prepared for the next phase of our evening, a libation ceremony, performed under the guidance of a friend connected to us by cell phone from dinner-hour San Francisco.

Toni Renée Battle is founder of the Legacy Project, a culture enrichment program for youth which emphasizes African American and Native American culture, tradition and histories. She had just met Joe that month and had not yet experienced a Slave Dwelling Project sleepover herself, though she was to take part in several over the next few years. I'd asked Toni about the act of pouring libation for the spirits of the people who had lived in the Bush-Holley House slave quarters, and what she would suggest we use and do.

Libation merely refers to the pouring of a liquid, often blessed in some way, to honor a deity or the spirits of the deceased. It is a ceremony older than the Greece and Rome in which it was a daily commonplace, with mention in the Bible and records of libation ceremonies in ancient Egypt. Indeed, Africa is where the ceremony still has an important place across a variety of cultures, and it was an African-inspired libation that Toni suggested. "Take the water," she told me, "and each of you pour some of it out, in the name of whoever means the most to you—could be a past enslaved person, it could be a special teacher in your life, it could be an abstract concept like racial reconciliation. Doesn't matter—you just have to mean it." "And then, what?" I asked. "Well," she said, "then you let spirit move you." I needed spirit now, if for no other reason than to quell the storm which threatened to block whatever I was capable of learning from this experience.

My three compatriots in tonight's slave dwelling sleepover had all agreed that we should do something special before we headed upstairs to the room over the kitchen, and all agreed that Toni's libation was the right thing. And all agreed when we located what felt like just the right place.

Outside the kitchen wing, we found a budding fruit tree, a cloud of white blooms hovering in the darkness. We stood beneath it, poured libation, then took each others' hands and spoke in honor of the people who had lived, worked and died here and in all the slave quarters up and down the eastern seaboard and across the South, those abandoned and gone and those still, by some miracle, standing, waiting for Joe to bring a light to their abandoned spaces, a voice to their silenced hearts.

I had carried into the quarters a few objects besides my toothbrush and pillow. One was a letter, written in 1939 by my great-great-grandmother, Elizabeth Mason, my link to New England slavery. Another was a letter from Nina. Most important of all, I brought a several page list I'd created giving the names of every African American and Native American person I then knew, whom my ancestors, South and North, had held in bondage.

For the libation, I had intended to speak to the memory of Candice Bush, whose home we would be dwelling in that night. But when it came time for me to pour the water, something else happened—in fact, to be perfectly honest, something came over me, which Toni later delightedly confirmed as "Spirit!" What came to me was the memory of Rose Jackson.

Standing under the flowering branches, I spoke to the good her love was still doing—that though she was placed in service to white people through no choice of her own, she made that service something sacred, a sacredness that was still going on, like the tides at Saybrook and the sweet incense of age and intimacy that pervaded the Bush-Holley House slave quarters, overcoming the bitterness that lived beside it. I spoke to Rose and to my respect for her, and when I said "ashé" with the others—a Yoruba word meaning "energy of the universe"—as Toni had instructed us, it was as if Rose had said "ashé" too.

Having completed the blessing, Joe, Dionne, Dave and I walked past priceless art works in the main house, ascended to the unadorned quarters over the kitchen, and unrolled our sleeping bags in that spare, chilly, creaking space, the shingles overhead rattling under sudden rain showers that continued throughout the night.

Because of the fragility of the floors, Debra Mecky had asked that only two of us sleep in the actual quarters, the other two on a viewing platform raised about a foot above the floor, located near the attic door. Joe and I took the space in the quarters, while Dionne and Dave took the viewing platform. We talked a bit, somewhat subdued after the evening's events. We were all about to turn in when Joe's cell phone rang.

"Hi Toni," Joe said. "We're just about to... what's that? You want to talk to Grant?" I could hear her voice even from across the room (Joe having advised that I sleep at some distance from his snoring if I wanted to get any rest that night). "You don't? Then, what...." I heard her talking, rapidly, excitedly. "OK, I'll tell him. OK, goodnight."

"That was Toni," Joe said. We all sat up to listen. "Funny, I don't believe in this stuff, as you know. But she wants me to tell you something, Grant. She says there's a woman spirit here—an older black woman—who has come to be near you tonight. Didn't say who." He chuckled a bit. "Anyway, that's all. She said, 'Tell Grant, he'll know.' Do you know what she's talking about?"

I shook my head, and we turned out the light.

But I did know.

I experienced an intense awareness of my surroundings, as if I suddenly understood just where I was, for the first time on this journey. I felt very far from familiar surroundings. I felt the distance in years from when Nina had lived, and suddenly wanted her near me. I also felt other things. I had a bitter sense of what life in this space had been like for the enslaved. I sensed the lack of any privacy from the master and mistress of the house—even though it was night, might a summons come from downstairs? Was it ever really bedtime for a slave? I saw what it might be like to live in conditions in which my life was controlled at every stage of experience, just as my market value was determined by those same forces. I knew the desolation even the lifelong enslaved knew at realizing they could do nothing to change their situation or the situation of their family. Love and luck had stepped in for Guy Drock, but not for most of the people my New England ancestors held in slavery. Not for Nan, enslaved to the Denisons, her half-Indian child conscripted to work off a sentence he had done nothing to deserve. Not for Embar, her long life spent looking after the Leffingwells.

I wondered, too, about those white people sleeping below me in the beautifully appointed rooms, with the highboys and feather beds and Persian carpets under their feet. Did they ponder the black bodies above? One of the most striking fugitive slave narratives published by Bostonian Benjamin Drew in 1856 is that of escaped slave John Little. How could enslavers, asked Little, "who know they are abusing others all day, lie down and sleep quietly at night...when they know that men feel revengeful, and might burn their property, or even kill them?" I felt that revenge in the attic, that fear in the bedchambers below.[8]

---

[8] Drew, *The Narratives of Fugitive Slaves in Canada*, 223.

It had been an incredibly busy couple of days, during which I had not had much rest. When I lay back down I finally began to drift off, regardless of the hard floor beneath me. As I drifted off, I pondered one more image—the presence of the woman Toni had called Joe about. And I knew it was Rose Jackson, "Faithful ever in all things". I know I was dreaming. Maybe it was the rain pattering overhead, the strange shadows. The rational part of me tells me that was the context. But I did see Rose Jackson, watching over us from within the darkness—secure in peace we still sought, which she long ago had found.

Three years and over three thousand miles later, in another city beside the sea—Seattle, Washington—on a May day brilliant with sunshine reflecting off glossy green leaves, and I sat in a car parked in front of First Presbyterian Church on 8th Avenue.

In the driver's seat, her elegant profile crisply poised against the shimmering world outside, was Dr. Lora-Ellen McKinney, a writer, dancer, child psychologist and, like me, an indefatigable hiker on the genealogist's pilgrimage trail.

The elderly man in the passenger seat whom she gazed at, focusing on every word, was her father, 88-year-old Rev. Dr. Samuel Berry McKinney. Rev. McKinney had been at the forefront of the civil rights battle in the 1960s, during my toddler years when I saw violence on TV. that I couldn't understand and which adults couldn't explain.

A classmate and colleague of the Rev. Dr. Martin Luther King, Jr., Rev. McKinney had convinced Dr. King to make what was his sole visit to the Pacific Northwest in November 1961, a trip which began with fanfare, was nearly derailed by circumstances more reminiscent of Selma, Alabama, than the liberal west coast, but which ultimately triumphed, at the same time exposing a racism alive and well hundreds of miles away from its presumed epicenter in the Deep South—a fact of Pacific Northwest history (and of its complex social dynamics in the present day) that, like slavery in Nina's family, seems to need to be re-membered again and again.

Like the televised violence I had been unable to fathom as a child, I was puzzled by the fact that Seattle, bastion of liberal thought and practice, had ever had need of a civil rights leader at all, let alone that Dr. King had come here and received a welcome that didn't jibe with the city's modern-day reputation.

This great man, his voice almost a whisper as he described the excitement and stress of those November days over half a century before, was my cousin, through a link neither of us knew about until DNA testing prompted Lora-Ellen to reach out to me.

With that welcoming gesture had come another lesson for me in debunking the myth which, like slavery in New England, wrongly claimed that racism itself was a phenomenon geographically fixed somewhere in the Deep South.

And had offered me, at the same time, the opportunity to choose peace with my past, if I wanted it. I already knew that peace wanted *me*.

I don't pretend to understand everything about autosomal DNA, the type used by 23andMe to identify matches between people who have tested with their service.

I just know that after my test results went live on the program's site, displaying my DNA matches—that is, everyone sharing DNA at or above the company's matching threshold of 7 centimorgans (cM)—I began to notice that a number of my matches who chose to include their photograph on their public internet profile were people of color. The program's differentiation indicated that my African American DNA cousins were connected to me on my mother's side, the side where as I knew by now there had been slavery in nearly every antebellum generation.

This of course brought to mind images I had not pondered or had simply chosen to ignore. I knew rape of black women by white men was the most common of crimes during the slavery era and after, because like slavery itself, such a violation was well within the rights of the white people who committed it. "The rape of black women by white men continued, often unpunished, throughout the Jim Crow era," writes Danielle L. McGuire. "As the acclaimed freedom fighter Fannie Lou Hamer put it, 'A black woman's body was never hers alone.'"[1] It could be said that for most of recorded history, no woman's body, whatever color, was her own. When I was in my early teens, Nina told me something her mother Eliza had confided to her, which her mother Amaryntha Culpepper Kelly had whispered to her—that on a ride in the country with her husband Arthur, Amma had been raped by him. They were both past middle age, and she had borne Arthur several children, one after the other, during their fifty-five years of marriage. Neither Eliza nor Nina speculated, at least to me, what had led to this. The shock of the rape, confided to a daughter about her father by her mother for reasons easy to understand but difficult to condone, and then by that daughter to *her* daughter, and by that daughter to her grandson, demonstrates the durability of memory coupled with pain. If this was the case for my family, in which the individuals involved were descended from white enslavers who had raped enslaved black women, enslavers whose wives might be vulnerable to rape within their marriage but never to assaults by any man who wanted

---

[1] McGuire, *At the Dark End of the Street*, xviii. Through 23andMe I have found African American cousins through my father's side as well. These links likely came through branches of my father's paternal Scottish and maternal German ancestral tree emigrating to colonial America in the eighteenth century, as was the case with my mother's German and Swiss ancestors. Interestingly, we know of one forebear, my fourth great-grandfather Andrew Doig (1756-1847), who was in Jamaica in 1802 and perhaps for some time afterward. It is certainly possible that Andrew could have left children by one or more Jamaican black women. I am digging more deeply into this history.

them, whose bed could be visited by the master or his sons or visiting male guests, by the overseer or white underlings, how much more indelible, crushing, generationally debilitating was the trauma of enslaved black women who were forced to submit and enslaved black men who were rendered impotent to intervene?

Just at the time I had started my genealogical quest, the issue of whether Thomas Jefferson, author of the Declaration of Independence and third United States President, had fathered children on a slave woman named Sally Hemings, was bubbling to the surface of American public consciousness and conscience, and finally proven by DNA testing.

Along with antebellum enslavers, overseers or even white men visiting a given plantation had ample opportunity to take advantage of enslaved women who could not fight back. Sometimes, as in the Jefferson-Hemings story, Hollywood's history would have us believe what master and slave shared was a "romance".

It is in no way impossible for there to have been such sentiments on one side or the other, between a man who held power and a woman who held none. After all, most women, including white ones, held no power anyway in that man's world. But chances are slim that in the eighteenth century in which the DNA data suggested so many of my African American links had their origin, love had anything to do with the impregnations that occurred. My imagination had thus far wandered into many dark corners of my ancestors' complicity in slavery, but not into historical beds or barns or attics where seed was planted by force, with pain and power, leaving me and my African American cousins to look each other in the eye (if we could) in the twenty-first century. Based on probability, I could have countless such cousins living today, each one a reminder of the system white America, North and South, had used to exploit more than just free labor—to colonize and conquer black women's bodies and through them to add to a store of slaves and wealth.

23andMe allows users to contact DNA cousins to share information, documentation, or ideas about how you may be related, or to discover a long-lost branch of the family or even a sibling, aunt, or uncle you had never heard of.

I sent out queries to cousins identified by the program. Often there was no reply, for reasons I could understand. Sometimes there was keen interest in locating our most recent common ancestor, only for our efforts to dwindle as it became clear we were seeking somebody we will probably never find in rooms where the light will never be turned on.

Not long after my testing results were made public to other 23andMe subscribers, Dr. Lora-Ellen McKinney of Seattle sent me a request to share genome information for herself and her father, Rev. Samuel Berry McKinney. "My father is quite excited to learn of you, given how helpful you might be at helping us figure out who may have enslaved the McKinneys," Lora-Ellen emailed me. "And, as you are not far away from Seattle, it is possible that we might meet at some point. He's 87, so sooner is better than later."[2]

Though DNA matching can verify shared ancestry, the circumstances under which black and white blood mixed provides few instances of documentation. After comparing data, Lora-Ellen and I spent the next several months playing rounds of the intellectually stimulating but not very productive game of educated guess. Such is the obstacle of the year 1870, the first United States census accounting for African American families.

---

[2] Dr. Lora-Ellen McKinney to author, 8 Apr 2014.

Even then, we found ourselves at either end of a spectrum of inchoate possibilities. Where Lora-Ellen ran into that wall trying to go back in time to identify, if she could, her enslaved ancestors, I hit it going forward in my attempts to trace descendants of my ancestors' freed slaves. Thinking we might make more progress if we pooled our thoughts and resources in per-son, I invited Lora-Ellen to spend Boxing Day weekend with me at my home in British Columbia.

Though not much older than myself, Lora-Ellen brought a hint of an earlier generation—of my grandmother, Nina. Tall, svelte, with an eastern seaboard angularity to her speech, Lora-Ellen physically couldn't have been more different from my grandmother. The similarities were in little things, like her sudden quiet statements summing up a moment's gravity or absurdity—sometimes both—in just a few words. Or the way Lora-Ellen sat listening to me with her jaw cradled against her open left hand, her right hand under her left elbow, her head at a certain angle, a combination that a grandson of Nina would recognize.

I also sensed Nina in Lora-Ellen's calm center, even when we talked about difficult topics. It was as if she, like my grandmother, had a special inner gyroscope keeping the heart level, whatever disturbed its equilibrium.

Lora-Ellen used that equilibrium almost as soon as she arrived. "While I very much appreciate your wish not to add to the burdens of blackness," she told me, "this equation changes within the context of a healthy relationship. It is fine for you to lean on me. I would expect that you will do the same for me. Relationships must have balance; it would be unfair and unsettling for me to do all of the leaning."[3]

---

[3] Dr. Lora-Ellen McKinney to author, July 2, 2015.

Wrapped in quilt by firelight, my cousin told me the story of her father's long, brave life. Samuel Berry McKinney was born on December 28, 1926 not in the South but in Flint, Michigan, son of the Rev. Wade Hampton McKinney and Ruth Berry. His original intention was not to be a preacher like his father. He noted in an interview years later how he and his friends, fellow preacher's son Martin Luther King, Jr., would do whatever they could to escape the "hot air" of the religious conventions they attended with their fathers. He wanted to be a lawyer in service to the civil rights fight which his father engaged from his pulpit. Samuel attended Morehouse College in Atlanta, alongside King, and like him he too would ultimately enter the ministry. Samuel went on to Colgate Rochester Divinity School, graduating in 1952 (receiving his Doctor of Ministry Degree in 1975), then served as pastor of the Olney Street Baptist Church in Providence, Rhode Island. Olney Street Baptist had spun off from Congdon Street Baptist Church, a historic black church dating to 1819, in 1901.

Rev. McKinney's next appointment brought him to Seattle in 1958, as a period of racial turmoil was engulfing the South. His congregation at Mount Zion Baptist Church was small, comprising around eight hundred members. As with the loaves and fishes of an earlier congregation, he was to double and triple that number as Mount Zion became not just a place to worship but a sanctuary for those in need, whether of food for "the least, the last, the lost, the locked up and the left out."[4] And the church became his springboard for significant influence on the stage of the civil rights and human rights movement, nationally and locally. Lora-Ellen told me her father had marched with Dr. King in Washington, D.C. in 1963 and in Selma and Montgomery in 1965.

---

[4] Author's meeting with Rev. McKinney in Seattle, WA on 10 May 2015.

"He was very active with CORE [Congress of Racial Equality], to open the job market to black people, and the NAACP, and the Urban League," she explained. "He was all about equal opportunities for people of color in a wide spectrum of areas—jobs, education, housing, everything. He founded the first black-owned bank in the city's history. He got himself arrested at the South African consul's house in Seattle, as part of an anti-apartheid protest." This information was exciting to know, giving me as it did another unexpected link to a warrior of the civil rights movement during its most critical years. But it also exposed big gaps in my education and experience. Racial inequality in friendly, inclusive Seattle?

I knew something of what had happened to Washington's Native American inhabitants. Where white people settled, indigenous peoples were cleared, often from areas they had occupied for untold centuries. This was the story of how all my American ancestors, from North to South, had made their mark on the landscape and, with backing from the government, seized lands that had belonged to other people. I also knew about the exclusionary laws imposed on certain areas of Seattle to restrict where non-white people could live. Neighborhoods had been declared off limits for Asians and blacks, with the exception of those who worked in domestic service there.

Still, hadn't a great deal changed since then? I asked Lora-Ellen. Seattle had never been a place where blacks had been prevented from eating at lunch counters or made to use separate facilities and drinking fountains. Hadn't Rev. McKinney brought Dr.. Martin Luther King, Jr. to the area in the city 1960s? Wasn't he welcomed and weren't Seattle's county, King, and an almost two mile stretch of roadway, named for him, not to mention a stretch of road named for Rev. McKinney himself?

As I finished, I saw I had a lot to learn. Lora-Ellen simply said quietly, "You won't understand it till you meet Daddy. But I can tell you, there was a lot of work to be done then— and there *is* a lot of work to be done today. I'll let him tell you the story when you see him."

The year Rev. McKinney took over Mount Zion Baptist in Seattle was an eventful one for Dr. Martin Luther King, Jr.

In summer 1958, Dr. King joined other civil rights leaders to meet with President Eisenhower. That fall, his first book, *Stride Toward Freedom: The Montgomery Story*, was published, and not long after while signing copies of the book in New York, King was almost stabbed to death by Izola Curry, mentally ill daughter of black sharecroppers from King's native Georgia, who nursed delusions about the civil rights leader. As the future would prove, Izola Curry would be the least of Dr. King's troubles, but this time, he survived.

In the next few years, he traveled to India, homeland of his hero, Mahatma Gandhi, whose portrait always hung in his office. In between meetings with John F. Kennedy, both as senator and as newly elected president, King became assistant pastor to his father, the Rev. Martin Luther King, Sr., at the latter's Atlanta congregation, Ebenezer Baptist, and devoted more and more of his time and talents to the fight against racial segregation. Violence toward Freedom Riders in Alabama took Dr. King to Montgomery in May 1961, where he spoke to anti-segregation demonstrators in a church that was being threatened by mobs. If King's speech was the poetry that conflict always drew from his pen, it was also angry, direct, deliberate. "Among the many sobering lessons that we can learn from the events of the past week," he thundered, "is that the Deep South will not impose limits on itself. The limits must be imposed from without."[6] These words echoed the struggles of the 1950s, when Federal troops had to be sent South to enforce integration and ensure fair voting practices, and were a presage of the pressure the Federal government would need to exert on the South to enforce equality legislation in the twenty-first century.

Rev. McKinney wanted his old friend to come to Seattle for a specific reason, to give a talk as part of a lecture series he had founded at Mount Zion Baptist which drew some of the brightest lights of the cause of civil rights and freedom for all. He also wanted Dr. King to publicly address issues around racism in a town which had a big problem in that area, though few were willing or able to admit it. "A lot of people thought it was better than it was," Rev. McKinney told a reporter in 1994. "It was better than some of the places many African Americans came from, but it certainly wasn't the promised land. On the surface it looked good, but you could detect more subtle strains of racism." Lora-Ellen told me she still has vivid memories of growing up in the household of a civil rights leader. "In the evenings after I had gone to bed – 7:30 PM – very serious looking men in suits and ties would enter the house through the front door," recalled Lora-Ellen of the confusion and comedy of life as the daughter of a civil rights leader. "My father was so busy and that I saw him so rarely, even though I sometimes heard him, that I named him my 'on again, off again, gone again Daddy.' My mother informed me that he was doing important work."[5]

Offering Dr. King a speaking fee and all expenses paid, Rev. McKinney organized every detail of the visit, which was to commence on Thursday, November 8. On November 6, McKinney wrote to King in Atlanta that he had arranged for

---

[5] "Martin Luther King Jr. and the Global Freedom Struggle": https://kinginstitute.stanford.edu/king-papers/documents/dexter-avenue-baptist-church-1.

a press conference in Seattle on the Thursday morning, and that he had tried his best to organize King's flight from Portland so as to give him some part of a night's sleep to catch up before the events unfolded in Seattle. Rev. McKinney also gave King fair warning of the situation into which he was about to step. "An extreme conservative right-wing element, whose presence is a known factor on the west coast, have been quite vocal about your coming," McKinney wrote. "The total community, which far exceeds the Negro population at 27,000 is quite aroused over some incidents that have occurred relative to your visit here. We have worked exceedingly hard to gain city-wide support for your first visit to the Pacific Northwest."[6]

One of the incidents referred to was that members of Rev. McKinney's congregation experienced harassment. "Over the course of the following month," wrote Ferdinand de Leon of the *Seattle Times*, "McKinney said he received several phone calls, threatening harm to King, and to McKinney and his family." Mount Zion congregation members reported being harassed by anonymous notes left for them at their workplaces.[7] It was never clear whether there were Klan connections behind some or all of this harassment, but it wasn't beyond possibility, especially as the Klan, as I found to my surprise, had once been as powerful a presence in 1920s Washington as it had in Oregon. "Finding few blacks at which to aim their venom in the pre-World War II Northwest," wrote Lornet Turnbull, "the white supremacists

---

[6] The King Center, letter from Rev. Samuel Berry McKinney to Martin Luther King, Jr. Regarding Travel Arrangements to Seattle, Monday, November 6, 1961.

[7] De Leon, "When King was in town," *The Seattle Times*, January 16, 1994, L1, 4 .

here focused instead on the Roman Catholic church and on foreigners."[8]

While the number of black residents was relatively small before the war, war work and the propulsion of the Great Migration brought Southern blacks to what they assumed would be a land of opportunity and freedom but which in reality offered familiar touches of the racist society they'd fled. Aside from the exclusionary covenants restricting property purchases and whole swathes of the job market closed to black people, there were more personal examples of that racism which Rev. McKinney perceived just below the surface. "I knew that black people had hard lives and that Martin Luther King was trying to help make everybody's lives easier," Lora-Ellen told me. "I heard my father and these men, for they were mainly men, talking about Seattle's most challenging issues. I recall them talking about access to funeral parlors and graveyards, about schools and jobs."[11] There was a meanness to this discrimination toward the dead. "McKinney remembers that Washell Cemetery segregated the black infants in its Babyland section," wrote de Leon.[9]

In 1961, Mount Zion occupied a much smaller church than today. Rev. McKinney had estimated that attendance might reach or top three thousand. With the World's Fair approaching and buildings all over the city closed for renovations or repairs, there was no religious property sufficient to hold that kind of crowd except for First Presbyterian Church on 8th Avenue. McKinney thus made arrangements that August before the scheduled lecture to use First Presbyterian and then began to advertise the event. It was at this

---

8 Turnbull, "A little Ku Klux Klan history" (published November 14, 2008): https://www.seattletimes.com/seattle-news/uw-project-sheds-light-on-ku-klux-klan-as-force-in-the-state.

9 Dr. Lora-Ellen McKinney to author, July 4, 2015.

point, before Dr. King had even set foot in town, that First Presbyterian chose to pull out of the agreement. The committee in charge claimed that their sanctuary was only to be used for religious meetings, not the type of lecture McKinney was advertising. Clerk Arthur E. Simon also stated that First Presbyterian was unhappy that lecture costs were being covered by Mount Zion via solicited donations, though this was done so the public could attend free of charge. "I asked if we could meet with the presbytery," Rev. McKinney told me. "We did, with the head of the presbytery, not the ministry. He was about six feet two or three, with a flowing mane of white hair. He was an officer in the church and he also had a political office. He had a voice that could put fear in both judge and jury. I told the people at First Presbyterian that they had not done right by us and I wasn't going to be quiet about it, and that I would tell the truth, the whole truth, and nothing but the truth, so help me God."[10]

This didn't faze the presbytery, but as the news that Mount Zion and Dr. King had been left in the lurch spread throughout the city, there was decided reaction. "The Christian Friends for Racial Equality criticized the cancellation," wrote de Leon. "And Robert B. Shaw, pastor of the Grace Methodist Church, called it 'the most deplorable action by any Christian church in Seattle in many years.'"[11]

"We then met with the people of Eagles Hall," Rev. McKinney explained, "put money down and that's where we had Dr. King give his talk. And we filled the auditorium. In fact, my wife almost didn't make it to hear him because we couldn't get a babysitter for our daughters—everybody wanted to be at the Eagles Auditorium. We had a reception

---

[10] Rev. Dr. Samuel Berry McKinney to author, May 10, 2015. McKinney remembers that Washell Cemetery segregated black infants…

[11] De Leon, "When King was in town," *The Seattle Times*, January 16, 1994, L1, 4.

at Plymouth United Church of Christ, who only charged us $30—somebody in the congregation paid the extra amount for the cleanup cost." Despite the controversy or even because of it, the air was alive with excitement, as Lora-Ellen recalls. "Every black person seemed simultaneously excited and happy and frightened," she said. "I also recall that I seemed to be the only child who knew anything about this. King came to our house. He brought a book about his life and read it to me as a bedtime story. I knew that this was an historic movement in my life."[12]

Despite the unexpected battle required to make it happen, the event was a success, and would lead to another resolution, postponed by many decades, which was what Rev. McKinney had wanted to tell me about as we sat in his car in front of First Presbyterian Church some fifty-three years later.

"Just before I retired in 1998," Rev. McKinney told me, "I got a letter in the mail. I looked at the envelope. It said 'First Presbyterian Church'. I just filed it quickly in the circular file. But something told me to go back and look at it because there wasn't a label on it—it had my name and address specifically. So I opened it." The letter had been written by the Rev. Winston R. Hull II, installed at First Presbyterian in 1997. "He wrote to apologize for the mistreatment that his church had imposed on our church," said Rev. McKinney.

McKinney called Hull and asked if there was a time when he could meet with him. Hull expressed interest but said it was for him to come to Mount Zion Baptist to meet with Rev. Mc-Kinney, not the other way around. During their conversation, according to Rev. McKinney, "he offered one for what had happened in 1961, and I accepted." For the remainder of Rev. McKinney's time as head of Mount Zion,

---

[12] Dr. Lora-Ellen McKinney to author, July 4, 2015.

he enjoyed a good relationship with First Presbyterian, and Rev. Hull was invited to speak at his retirement reception, during which he read from the letter which had led to the rapprochement.

Rev. McKinney, Lora-Ellen and I had earlier talked a lot about our mysterious yet all too clear genetic link. I had felt especially hesitant about this in Rev. McKinney's presence, and as I pondered what or whether to say, I recalled a scene in *Traces of the Trade*.

In the documentary, several white DeWolf descendants are sitting in a circle debating the pros and cons of the trip they have taken together to the places where their ancestors had enslaved African people. One of the group, Elly Hale, begins to cry. She sees Juanita Moore, the film's African American producer, standing off to one side observing this conclave of liberal white angst, as if exiled outside its sacred circle but forced by conventions nobody dares ignore to bear witness to it. For Elly, however, it was as if Juanita had been made invisible, like the black nanny many in the room had known as children, who in any case their ancestors— and mine—had known for hundreds of years, waiting on the moods of troubled white folks, drying tears and lending a shoulder, her autonomy and individuality entirely conscripted to ensuring white comfort. I thought of all the enslaved women in my family history, their powerlessness a strange, discordant music played against strong, reassuring voices that soothed many a white child of my blood down the centuries, whose names—Rose, Charity, Phebe, Vinia— were like music, too. And I thought of Mrs. Daniel, Nina's Aunt Sammy, no slave but her life just as circumscribed in the Jim Crow South of Nina's girlhood, a woman whose safety was precarious in that South yet whose presence in Nina's house ironically seemed to center a troubled world. Ultimately, in the documentary, Elly invites Juanita, who appears increasingly angry, to sit with her and the others in the circle. She asks Juanita for her opinion of the many troubled and troubling questions the DeWolfs have unearthed in the course of filming, as they visit all the sites of their family's inhumanity. Tearless and honest, Juanita finally replies, "We've been taking care of you for centuries and we're sick and tired of taking care of you." The silence that followed was filled with more meaning than any amount of vocalized white grief could ever create.[13]

My DNA and my McKinney cousins' DNA contained markers of shared blood, not some unavoidable programming developed over the centuries that gave me permission to seek solace in them, whether or not they wished to give it, to lean on them, whether or not they could bear it. I, too, was sick of demanding that I be taken care of.

Writing of the DeWolf descendants' trip to Ghana, Tom DeWolf describes a festival they attended. One of the group approached a Ghanaian man who was performing what seemed to be a ritual cleansing. The man took leaves which he had wet in a river and brushed them over the bodies of other Ghanaians. Tom's cousin asked the man if he would perform the ritual for him. The Ghanaian man said no. "He said we needed to deal with our own issues and then have our own white elders perform a cleansing ceremony for us," wrote Tom.[14]

I had had no white elders to approach, and I didn't want their blessing. I didn't believe in blessings. I believed in accepting responsibility, which Nina had conditioned me to take on as she took it on; which I took on because I, too, knew we must never forget that my family had once used other human beings like draft animals: that thanks to slaves

---

[13] *Traces of the Trade: A Story from the Deep North*, Katrina C. Browne, director, 2008

[14] DeWolf, *Inheriting the Trade*, 143-144.

who worked in fields under hot sun and threat of a whip, my ancestors had the cash to buy their children books; that thanks to slaves who cooked and cleaned for them, my ancestors had had the leisure to teach their children to read them; that thanks to enslaved women who could not say no, my male ancestors increased their human inventory, at the same time leading me to this moment, sitting in a car in Seattle with my cousins, our blood joined through my ancestors' violence toward theirs.

I said, "Rev. McKinney, I have spoken of this before to Lora-Ellen. I have to say it to you, too. As much as I love that we have found one another, I wish it wasn't because of what my people did to yours. If I could just go back in time and stop what my ancestors did to yours, I would. Even if it meant we were not sitting here now and never knew each other at all."

Though he was getting up in years, and easily tired, Rev. McKinney had the soft, receptive, keen eyes of a much younger man, and the quicksilver quality of response, too. He looked at me with both affection and humor, and put a hand over mine. "The sins of your fathers are not yours to carry," he said quietly but firmly, in a tone meant to inform me that this would be the last time he would have to tell me something so basic, so obvious. "Doing good is as much about work as it is prayer. Keep doing good work, and leave the ancestors to work out the destinies they made for themselves."

In *The Souls of Black Folk*, W.E. B. Du Bois wrote:

> Between me and the other world there is ever an unasked question: unasked by some through feelings of delicacy; by others through the difficulty

of rightly framing it. All, nevertheless, flutter round it. They approach me in a half-hesitant sort of way, eye me curiously or compassionately, and then, instead of saying directly, How does it feel to be a problem? they say, I know an excellent colored man in my town; or, I fought at Mechanicsville; or, Do not these Southern outrages make your blood boil? At these I smile, or am interested, or reduce the boiling to a simmer, as the occasion may require. To the real question, How does it feel to be a problem? I answer seldom a word.[15]

My journey through the murky waters of my slave-owning ancestry had asked that same question of me: How does it feel to be a problem?

I recalled my surprise at arriving in Norwich to meet descendants of a black person enslaved by my white ancestors, and finding they looked no different from me. But was this about color? Was it not about something deeper than skin? Words of Ta-Nehisi Coates ran through my head: "perhaps being named 'black' was just someone's name for being at the bottom, a human turned to object, object turned to pariah."[16]

Beyond names, words, labels, descriptors official and vernacular, was this what my American ancestors, your American ancestors, were, are, most complicit in? Person turned pariah?

I do know that at the end of my journey, sitting in a car on a Seattle street with Rev. McKinney—blood of my blood and bone of my bone—outside the church which had rejected him, whose rejection he approached with love and whose

---

[15] Du Bois, *The Souls of Black Folk*, 2-3.

[16] Coates, *Between the World and Me*, 55.

apology he refused to throw away, I had learned that I was still at the beginning of what Lora-Ellen aptly termed my "journey to genealogical redemption." But this wasn't about asking for forgiveness, any more than it was about apologizing. Nobody can apologize for a crime four centuries old. But as Rev. McKinney reminded me, we can do something now about its after effects. All of us who benefit from the institution of slavery yet do not acknowledge it, whether we are Southern or Northern, descended from slave-owners or recent immigrants to this nation, are part of the problem— the problem not just of forgetting, but of remembering without learning. We are also the solution. The sins of our fathers are not ours to carry. The ancestors must be allowed to take care of their destinies, on their own terms, in their own time, as Rev. McKinney told me. But we can help get about healing by doing good work in the now. And as Americans, we can become a remembering family.

AFTERWORD

Daryl D'Angelo

Families intersect with other families all the time. From marriages to neighbors to business dealings, we ebb and flow together and apart continually. Some of these encounters leave barely a scratch on life's surface, while others tear lives asunder and redirect futures.

Grant's ancestors' encounter with mine is certainly one of the latter. It's sometimes said that we're all a product of the past; it's seldom mentioned that the past has to be uncovered before it can be understood.

Following my Drock ancestors as far as the records allow took me through times and places and events I had never fully understood. The journey demanded that I abandon my identity and challenged the narratives and lore of my entire family. It brought my history books to life, and it taught me that most of what I knew was wrong.

More than once, the journey required an entire rethink of everything I thought I knew about ethnicity and slavery and American history. And in 2011 - when I thought the final chapter had been written and the final stone overturned — this remarkable family's history brought me Grant Hayter-Menzies.

Grant arrived in the Drock story initially as an email. He embodied extreme White Guilt and a need to Make Amends for the Evil Deeds of his Forebears, and at that point in my own journey, I couldn't think of a single reason why I would want to interact with him.

His Bushnell ancestor held Guy Drock (my 6x great-grand-father) in bondage, and used Guy's blacksmithing skills for his own enrichment. To my mind, the fact of that enslavement led to generations of hard-scrabble existence on marginal farms. I felt that the Bushnells and Leffingwells of the world were why my family was seen as "less than"; why their farms were disparagingly called "Drock neighborhood"; why they were described as "a bunch of mulattos" who were lazy and deservedly indigent. It's why the Drock Cemetery in Caneadea New York, filled with "blacks and Indians", today has no stones standing and cows graze in it.

I had spent more than a decade learning about my family and their travails and secrets and triumphs. I was sad for the deci-sions they'd felt they had to make to become successful in this world. The mere name of Grant's ancestor -- "Bushnell" -- made me grumpy. Researching in Hartford, CT meant I had to go through Bushnell Square, and I hated that. Why would I want to meet with the descendant of my family's enslavers? What did he want? Specifically, what did he want from me?

And yet... and yet.... I was intrigued. I was still on my learning journey, and the opportunity for understanding was enticing.

At the time Grant was part of a group called "Coming to the Table" - a bunch of folks with the interesting idea of bringing descendants of slave holders together with the descendants of those who had been enslaved by them. Don Roddy and I were his first successful contacts. Grant had found Don online and reached out, and Don then reached out to me with the news of this white guy who felt really bad about his slave-holding Connecticut ancestors and wanted to apologize.

A flurry of emails and some months later, I found myself driving down to Norwich, Connecticut to meet with both Grant and Don Roddy.

I was pretty sure he wasn't expecting us to look like... well... his white ancestors. I'd even emailed Don to ask whether Grant knew. Don said he thought so...?   But there we all were in the parking lot of the Leffingwell House, looking remarkably like one another. And it was quite clear that Grant had not known. He hadn't even suspected.

The entire scene was shocking for Grant, who I think was a bit lost for a while afterward.mLike Guy and Sarah Drock's descendants (like me, in fact), Grant had to abandon all his preconceptions of: New England; slavery in the North; ethnicity and miscegenation;   the one drop rule. This was terribly difficult for Grant to do, and we spent many hours across very late nights, "talking" the issues over electronically. To reconcile today with yesterday, he had to learn (and unlearn) legends and lore and media and political tendencies – just as I had. Tough stuff.

In our shared family story, nothing is quite as we were taught in school; everything is just slightly askew. It's like visiting a country where the language is the same but the differences in dialect are sharp enough to disorient. While based on the same institutional and legal concepts, slavery in the North was generally quite different, in practice, from slavery in the South. Yes, there were slave traders; the Leffingwells, for example, would fit into Charleston as neatly as Norwich. Yes, there were harsh laws and property ownership restrictions; one can't help but wonder at the conversations behind the property deed to Guy and Sarah Drock.

But the economy was not large-scale agrarian. There were certainly exceptions, but enslavers tended to have only one or two slaves, and they typically lived all together within the same four walls. Attic bedrooms often accommodated not just the enslaved, but white children of the owner as well. This different scale and familiarity led to a vastly different culture and experience from that of the south.

Understanding this past and how it impacted the trajectory of our families has been a fulfilling and wondrous journey. It was my great privilege to travel Grant's road in partial tandem. As he worked to exorcise his one-dimensional demons, he learned to let go of some of the anger, making way for a clearer view of the past.

Listening to Grant's heartfelt anguish and helping him find his emotional feet allowed unexpected exploration of my own pre-conceptions about his ancestors. It's one thing to grasp a concept theoretically, but it's another thing entirely to apply that theory to one's most personal history. Through our friendship, I came to understand that my family did not suffer specifically because of Benajah Bushnell and his Leffingwell wife. These branches of my family lived through over 200 years of policy and stigma and racism that cannot be attributed to a single person. That's too simplistic and flat. The Bushnells of the world were neither Satanic Evildoers nor Saviors. Through their charities and actions, they demonstrated that they were humane people living within the dictates of their historical mores and strict society.

Blaming them does nothing. It does not advance my family or their story; it does not increase understanding or historical awareness; it especially does not assuage anger or facilitate a harmonious future for our society.

As much as Grant wanted to make amends – to apologize for the actions of his ancestors – he couldn't. Not because I wouldn't have accepted them, but because he is not who inflicted the wounds, and it was not I who received them. Did my great-great grandfather struggle much harder than he had to because of his ethnicity? Yes. Did they lose farms and lumber mills because of racism? Ayup, it looks as if that's precisely what happened. Did my great-grandfather change his name and re-invent his family history to hide his enslaved ancestors? I suspect that's exactly why he did those things, yes. Just like almost every other branch of the family, they looked for a way forward for their children in a racist society. I hate that they were faced with such choices.

Can Grant change any of that? Absolutely not.

Uncovering and owning his ancestors, though, and acknowledging them as complex people who probably did some good things in their lives along with the hideous enslavement of human beings, gives us all a better picture of the world that was. Just as describing Grant as merely a "descendant of a slave-holder" does him a tremendous disservice, so too does narrowing the focus too tightly on our history. Grant is a far more valuable and worthy human being than such a narrow label allows, and in that sense, I suspect he's not too different from his ancestors.

Grant's family and mine collided in a profound and compelling manner. Their initial encounter nearly 300 years ago in a New England river town set the feet of their children on radically different paths that improbably led us to friendship and under-standing today.

Our shared history is the story of America. It's not an ideal place, and there is a great deal of pain and regret. There are (and will always be) questions without answers, but each of us is more than simply the product of our past. Like us, our ancestors were complex and three-dimensional. Our stories, society and history are far richer and more colorful than the flattened caricatures with which we've been presented. All of us just have to make the effort to look a little deeper.

ILLUSTRATIONS

Nina Lewis Strawser, the author's maternal grandmother, near San Bernardino, California, 1937.

Photo: Grant Hayter-Menzies

The baby dress mended by Mrs. Daniel, whom Nina knew as Aunt Sammy. Nina kept the dress through many moves and upheavals throughout her long life, and bequeathed it to me.

Photo: Grant Hayter-Menzies

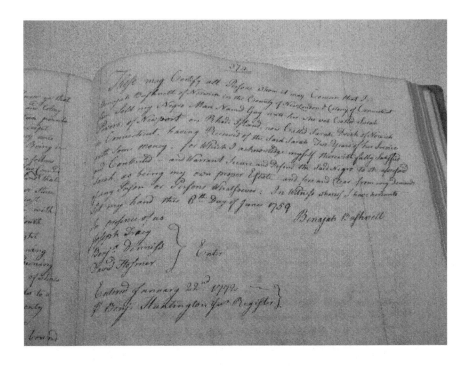

The 1759 bill of sale of Guy Drock, slave to Benajah Bushnell of Norwich, CT, in which Guy is sold to Sarah Powers, a Bushnell maidservant who was likely white, so she and Guy could marry.

Photo: Grant Hayter-Menzies

The Victorian façade of the eighteenth century house built by Guy Drock on land provided to him by the Bushnell family in Norwich, Connecticut.

Photo: Grant Hayter-Menzies

Group portrait of four of Guy Drock's descendants.

At back, from left, Guy's great- great-granddaughters Esther Chirkins-Ost and Mary Chirkins-Clemens. The two older ladies seated are believed to be, from left, Susannah Drock, Guy's great-granddaughter, and her mother, Esther Buel-Drock.

Photo: Donald Roddy
(used with permission)

At Norwich Free Academy discussing Guy Drock, Benajah Bushnell and slavery in Connecticut. From left: Grant Hayter-Menzies, Daryl D'Angelo, Donald Roddy.

Photo: Norwich Bulletin

The William Hart House in Old Saybrook, where Rose Jackson, enslaved as a girl, lived and worked most of her long life.

Photo: Grant Hayter-Menzies

In background, the Yale Boulder, and in foreground the marker indicating that the first iteration of Yale College, then the Collegiate School, stood near the spot. Nathaniel Lynde donated the lot on which the school was convened.

Photo: Grant Hayter-Menzies

The gravestone of Rose Jackson, Cypress Cemetery, Old Saybrook, Connecticut.

Photo: Grant Hayter-Menzies

The Lynde family plot in Cypress cemetery, Old Saybrook, Connecticut.

Photo: Grant Hayter-Menzies

Grave of Hannah Lynde Griswold, wife of the Rev. George Griswold of Lyme.

Hannah's father, brother, and nephews in Old Saybrook were enslavers; her husband, Rev. Griswold, who served with distinction for many years, owned an African slave named Cornelia. His father, too, owned slaves.

Photo: Grant Hayter-Menzies

Thomas Leffingwell's estate inventory, listing Robin at £50. Embar, described as being "past labor" (too old to work), may be included under the amount assigned to Robin, or the empty space may mean she was assigned no value at all. Note that, as in Southern inventories of a century later, the enslaved humans are listed after the livestock. Connecticut Wills and Probate Records,

The Leffingwell House, as reproduced in Mary Elizabeth Perkins' *Old Houses of the Antient Town of Norwich 1660-1800* (pub. 1895), prior to its removal to its current placement within the town of Norwich.

Reproduction: Grant Hayter-Menzies

The Leffingwell house today.
Right: The "north door" of the Leffingwell house, accessed through the basement level. According to Perkins, slave auctions were said to have taken place at this door.

Photo: Grant Hayter-Menzies

Bush-Holley House in Cos Cob, CT

The portion above the kitchen (windows with green shutters), just under the eaves, is the former slave quarters of the house.

Photo: Grant Hayter-Menzies

A view to the former slave quarters of Bush- Holley House. The author, along with Joseph McGill of the Slave Dwelling Project, writer Dionne Ford Kurtti, and the Rev. David Pettee, spent the night of March 30, 2012 in this space.

Photo: Grant Hayter-Menzies

The morning after our Slave Dwelling Project sleepover in Bush-Holley House. From left: Joseph McGill, Grant Hayter-Menzies, Dionne Ford Kurtti, and the Rev. David Pettee.

Photo: Grant Hayter-Menzies

The Rev. Dr. Samuel Berry McKinney, at left, with his former schoolmate and lifelong friend the Rev. Dr. Martin
Luther King, Jr.

Photo: Dr. Lora-Ellen McKinney
(used with permission)

The author, at left, in Seattle with the Rev. Dr. Samuel Berry McKinney, Sean William Menzies, Dr. Lora-Ellen McKinney, and Scout, May 2015.

Photo: Grant Hayter-Menzies

I have spent more than three decades researching my maternal grandmother's enslaver ancestors, compiling as much information as possible on the people they enslaved. As time goes on, I uncover more data, which means the following lists are not complete. In that sense, my quest may never end.

Enslaved people listed in the inventory of Parmelia Miller Wise, the author's fifth great-grandmother and widow of James Wise (1781-1858), at Colquitt, Louisiana on February 15, 1864.

- Judy
- Moses
- Sarah and her child:
- March
- Ginette and her children:
- Satin
- Oliver
- Buell
- Ginette
- Warren
- Warren G. ß
- Female

Source: February 15, 1864, Inventory and Appraisement of Estate of Parmelia Wise, widow of James Wise: Book of Inventories B, 543-44.

Enslaved people listed in the estate papers of the author's sixth great-grandfather George Lambright (1765-1835) at Copiah County, Mississippi on 25 Sep. 1835.

- Fany

- Assariah
- Lida
- Sam
- Prince
- Randall
- Harry
- Jack
- Charity
- Hannah and child
- Mary
- Phebe*
- Isabella

Source: Inventory reproduced (13-15) in Schertz, *The Lambrights: Descendants of Nicholas Lambright, a Revolutionary War Soldier.* Provo, UT: J. Grant Stevenson, 1977.

✳

People enslaved by the author's fifth great-grandfather George Lambright, Jr. (1798-1858) in Union Parish, Louisiana before 1850.
- Phebe* (*same as above?*) (sold to Martin Mims February 23, 1849)
- Littleton (sold to Thomas Van Hook December 8, 1851)
- NN (Charity?)
- NN
- NN

Sources: Union Parish Conveyance Book C, 109, February 23, 1849; Union Parish Conveyance Book D, 561, December 8, 1851.

Enslaved man listed in the will of the author's fourth great-grandfather Lemuel Culpepper (1785-1842), proved November 17, 1842 Jasper County, Georgia.
- Robert

Source: For Robert: "Culpepper Connections", Lemuel Culpepper: http://www.culpepperconnections.com/ss/p120.htm.

Enslaved man sold by Lemuel Culpepper to Jonas Holland of Jasper County, Georgia.
- Anderson Culpepper

Source: For Anderson: April 1842: Jasper Co., Georgia, Deed Book D, Page 2.

People enslaved by the author's fifth great-grandfather John Gaston (1770-1845) of Gaston County, North Carolina.
- Vinia
- Wallace (her son?)
- NN (child?)
- NN
- NN
- NN

Source: "North Carolina Estate Files, 1663-1979," database with images; Gaston County, North Carolina, wills 1663-1978; estate papers, 1839-1928, Gaston County > G > Gaston, John (1845) > image 2 of 26; State Archives, Raleigh.

Man enslaved by the author's seventh great-grandfather Col. Jonathan Latimer of Montville, Connecticut

- Cesar

Source: Brown and Rose, *Black Roots in Southeastern Connecticut, 1650-1900*, 5, 473.

Enslaved people purchased by the author's sixth great-grandfather Eusebius Bushnell (1747-1812) in Davidson County, Tennessee on August 29, 1789.
- Phil
- Yarro
- March

Source: "Tennessee Probate Court Books, 1795-1927," images, FamilySearch (https://familysearch.org/ark:/61903/3:2:77TV-TGVZ?cc=1909088&wc=M6QS-1N5%3A179633601%2C179633602 : 22 May 2014), Davidson > Inventories, Wills, 1784-1794, Vol. 01 > image 80 of 216; county courthouses, Tennessee.

Enslaved people sold by Eusebius Bushnell to Frederick Stump.
- Yarro
- March

Source: "Tennessee Probate Court Books, 1795-1927," images, FamilySearch (https://familysearch.org/ark:/61903/3:2:77TV-TGV2?cc=1909088&wc=M6QS-1N5%3A179633601%2C179633602 : 22 May 2014), Davidson > Inventories, Wills, 1784-1794, Vol. 01 > image 90 of 216; county courthouses, Tennessee.

❋

People enslaved by the author's ninth great-grandfather Nathaniel Lynde (1659-1729) of Old Saybrook, Connecticut, from his inventory taken on April 3, 1730.

- Juba
- Nero
- Cesar
- Rose

Source: Probate Packets, Linsley, D-Maltbie, N, 1719-1880, Filmstrip #1414; Connecticut State Library (Hartford, Connecticut); Probate Place: Hartford, Connecticut.

People enslaved by the author's eighth great-grandfather Benajah Bushnell (1681-1762) of Norwich, Connecticut.

- Robin
- Guy Drock

Sources: Guy: Norwich Land Records, New London County, Book 19, 374; Robin: Brown and Rose, 564.

People enslaved by the author's tenth great-grandfather Simon Lynde (1624-1687) of Boston, Massachusetts: "<u>ffour Negros</u>", unnamed, but if they were young people at Lynde's death they could be the four appearing in Nathaniel Lynde's inventory in 1729. Simon Lynde was active in the Indian slave trade as well. The Indian slaves bought and sold by him are not named or numbered, but we may assume they were many more than the "ffour Negros" listed below.

- Marea, "convict by her own confession in court of committing Fornication and having a bastard Childe,

the Court sentenc'd her to bee whip't with ten Stripes or to pay Forty Shillings in mony fine to the County" (Session of 24 April 1674, *Records of the Suffolk County Court*, Vol. XXX, 809).
- NN
- NN
- NN

Sources: For "ffour Negros": Suffolk County, MA, Probate Records, Volumes 13-14, 1688-1701, volume 13, 153; for involvement in Indian slavery, see Newell, *Brethren by Nature*, 181.

People enslaved by author's tenth great-grandmother Margaret (Locke) Taylor Willoughby Hammond (1634-1683) of Charlestown, Massachusetts: Three African slaves, unnamed.
- NN
- NN
- NN

Source: Lawrence Hammond inventory: "Good for what ails you: Vignettes From a Colonial Diary – Lawrence Hammond with some notes by Julie Helen Otto. *Nexus*, Vol. 6 (1989).

People enslaved by the author's eleventh great-grandfather Capt. George Denison (1620-1694) of Mystic, Connecticut.
- John (Native American, "bought of the county")
- Job (Native American, "born in this house")
- Female

- Nan and child. Nan "had illegitimate child by Indian Nemuck. The child was to serve Denison for 21 yrs., according to a decision of the ct., 1668."

Source: "Will of George Denison – 1693". *The New England Historical & Genealogical Register and Antiquarian Journal* (January 1859), Vol. 13, 73-77; Brown & Rose, *Black Roots in Southeastern Connecticut, 1650-1900*, 535.

People enslaved by the author's sixth great-grandfather John Griswold (1690-1764) of Lyme, Connecticut.
- Phillis
- Neptune
- Male
- Male

Sources: Salisbury, *Family-Histories and Genealogies*, 48 (Out of print – see: https://archive.org/details/familyhistories-g02sali); Brown and Rose, 539.

Woman enslaved by the author's eighth great-grandfather, Rev. George Griswold (1692-1761)
- Cornelia

Source: Brown & Rose, *Black Roots in Southeastern Connecticut, 1650-1900*, 482.

People enslaved by the author's ninth great-grandfather Thomas Leffingwell (1649-1724) of Norwich, Connecticut.
- Robin
- Embar

Source: Probate Packets, Lee, Elizabeth-Lester, John, 1675-1850, Case 3167, Filmstrip #1243; Connecticut State Library (Hartford, Connecticut); Probate Place: Hartford, Connecticut.

Ghanaian captives brought to London, England by the author's thirteenth great-grandfather Thomas Locke, with brother John Locke (Lok) (1555).
- 5 men, three of them named Binne, Anthonie and George, from Shama on the Gold Coast

When three of the five men were returned to Shama, the English who were present were astonished, not expecting, as Carole Levin writes, these "'savages' to have such emotions."

Sources: Costello, *Black Salt*, 2; Levin, *The Reign of Elizabeth I*, 119-120.

BIBLIOGRAPHY

Allis, Marguerite. *Connecticut River*, New York: G. P. Putnam's Sons, 1939.

Allyn, Adeline Bartlett. *Black Hall Traditions and Reminiscences*, Hartford: The Case, Lockwood & Brainard Company, 1908.

Ball, Edward. *Slaves in the Family*, New York: Farrar Straus Giroux, 1998.

Bennett, Lerone. *Before the Mayflower: A History of Black America*, New York: Penguin Books, 1988.

Berlin, Ira. *Many Thousands Gone: The First Two Centuries of Slavery in North America*, Cambridge: Belknap Press/Harvard University Press, 2000.

Blackmon, Douglas A. *Slavery by Another Name: The Re-Enslavement of Black Americans from the Civil War to World War II*, New York: Anchor, 2009.

Blassingame, John W. *The Slave Community: Plantation Life in the Antebellum South*, Oxford University Press, 1972.

Blight, David W. *A Slave No More: Two Men Who Escaped to Freedom, Including Their Own Narratives*, New York: Mariner, 2009.

Borque, Bruce J. *Twelve Thousand Years: American Indians In Maine*, Lincoln, NB: Bison Books/University of Nebraska Press, 2004.

Bostian, Mary L. Mason and Eva L. Bradley Cralle. *Kinship: It's All Relative* (unpublished history of the Mason family), compiler: Mary L. Mason Bostian, 1994.

Bradford, William. *Of Plimoth Plantation*, Boston: Wright & Potter Printing Co., 1898.

Brandow, James C. *Genealogies of Barbados Families*, from Caribbeana and The Journal of the Barbados Museum and Historical Society. Baltimore: Genealogical Publishing Company, 2001.

Brown, Barbara W. and James M. Rose. *Black Roots in South-eastern Connecticut, 1650-1900*, Detroit: Gale Research Company, 1980.

Bushnell, George Eleazer. *Bushnell Family Genealogy: Ancestry and Posterity of Francis Bushnell (1580 - 1646) of Horsham, England And Guilford, Connecticut Including Genealogical Notes of other Bushnell Families, whose connections with this branch of the family tree have not been determined,* Nashville, 1945. Available on line courtesy of the Connecticut General Assembly: https://www.cga.ct.gov/hco/books/Bushnell_Family_Genealogy.pdf.

Catchings, Fermine Baird. *Baird and Beard Families: A Genealogical, Biographical and Historical Collection of Data,* Nashville: Baird-Ward, 1918.

Caulkins, Frances Manwaring. *A History of Norwich: From Its Possession by the Indians to the Year 1866,* Hartford, 1866.

Chase, Jon, *Montville.* Mount Pleasant, SC: Arcadia Publishing, 2004.

Clinton, Catherine. *Tara Revisited: Women, War, and the Plantation Legend,* New York: Abbeville Press, 2013.

Coates, Ta-Nehisi. *Between the World and Me,* New York: Spiegel & Grau/Random House, 2015.

Costello, Ray. *Black Salt: Seafarers of African Descent on British Ships.* Liverpool: Liverpool University Press, 2012.

Cruson, Daniel. *The Slaves of Central Fairfield County: The Journey From Slave to Freeman in Nineteenth Century Connecticut,* Mount Pleasant, SC: The History Press, 2007.

Davis, Rev. B. F. *Lynchburg, VA and Nelson Co. VA (Wills, Deeds and Marriages 1807-1831),* Greeneville, SC: Southern Historical Press, 1985.

DeWolf, Thomas Norman and Sharon Leslie Morgan. *Gather at the Table: The Healing Journey of a Daughter of Slavery and a Son of the Slave Trade,* Boston: Beacon Press, 2013.

DeWolf, Thomas Norman. *Inheriting the Trade: A Northern Family Confronts Its Legacy as the Largest Slave-Trading Dynasty in U.S. History,* Boston: Beacon Press, 2009.

Di Bonaventura, Allegra. *For Adam's Sake: A Family Saga in Colonial New England*, New York: Liveright/W.W. Norton, 2014.

Dimancescu, Katherine. *The Forgotten Chapters: My Journey Into the Past*, Dimancescu 2013.

Drew, Benjamin. *The Narratives of Fugitive Slaves in Canada*, Toronto: Coles Publishing Company, 1981.

Du Bois, W.E.B. *The Souls of Black Folk*, edited by Henry Louis Gates, Jr. New York: Oxford University Press, 2007.

Farrow, Ann, Joel Lang and Jenifer Frank. *Complicity: How the North Promoted Prolonged and Profited from Slavery*, New York: Ballantine Books, 2005.

Finkelman, Paul, ed., *The Encyclopedia of African American History 1619-1895, From the Colonial Period to the Age of Frederick Douglas*, Vol. 2, 328.

Finkelman, Paul. *Slavery and the Founders: Race and Liberty in the Age of Jefferson*, New York: Routledge, 2000.

Fox-Genovese, Elizabeth,. *Within the Plantation Household: Black and White Women of the Old South*, Chapel Hill: University of North Carolina Press, 1988.

Gerzina, G. H. *Mr. and Mrs. Prince: How an Extraordinary Eighteenth Century Family Moved Out of Slavery and Into Legend*, New York: Amistad/Harper Collins, 2009.

Glasson, Travis. *Mastering Christianity: Missionary Anglicanism and Slavery in the Atlantic World*, Oxford University Press, 2011

Grayling, A. C. *Toward the Light of Liberty: The Struggles for Freedom and Rights That Made the Modern Western World*, New York: Walker Books, 2009.

Griswold, Mac. *The Manor: Three Centuries at a Slave Plantation on Long Island*, New York: Farrar Straus Giroux, 2013.

Hakluyt, Richard. *The Principal Navigations, Voyages, Traffiques, and Discoveries of the English Nation, The second voyage to Guinea set out by Sir George Barne, Sir John Yorke, Thomas Lok, Anthonie Hickman and Edward Castelin, in the yere 1554. The Captaine whereof was M. John Lok.* On line version, Perseus Digital Library, Tufts University, Gregory R. Crane, editor-in-chief: http://www.perseus.tufts.edu/hopper/text?doc=Perseus%3Atext%3A1999.03.0070%3Anarrative%3D522.

Haley, Alex. *Roots: The Saga of an American Family*, New York: Doubleday, 1976.

Hall, David D. *A Reforming People: Puritanism and the Transformation of Public Life in New England*, New York: Knopf, 2011.

Hall, Verne M. and Elizabeth B. Plimpton. *Vital Records of Lyme, Connecticut to the End of the Years 1850*, Lyme, CT: American Revolution Bicentennial Commission, 1976.

Horton, James Oliver and Lois E. Horton. *Slavery and the Making of America*, Oxford University Press, 2006.

Hubbard, Rev. William. *The History of the Indian Wars in New England: From the First Settlements to the Termination of the War with King Philip, in 1677*, Berwyn Heights, MD: Heritage Books, 2010.

Hughes, Thomas P. *American Ancestry: Giving the Name and Descent of Americans Whose Ancestors Settled In the United States Previous to the Declaration of Independence A.D. 1776*, Vol. 1, Albany: Joel Munsell's Sons, 1887.

Iyengar, Sujata. *Shades of Difference: Mythologies of Skin Color in Early Modern England*, Philadelphia: University of Pennsylvania Press, 2005.

Jacobs, Harriet, Jean Fagan Yellin, Editor. *Incidents in the Life of a Slave Girl, Written by Herself*, Cambridge: Harvard University Press, 1987.

Karlstrand, Lillian Bentley compiler, Lorraine Cook White, editor. *The Barbour Collection of Connecticut Town Records, Lyme 1667-1852*, Baltimore: Genealogical Publishing Company, 2000.

Lampos, Jim and Michaelle Pearson. *Remarkable Women of Old Lyme*, Charleston: The History Press, 2015.

Lancaster, Robert. *The Jungles of Arkansas: A Personal History of the Wonder State*, Fayetteville: University of Arkansas Press, 1989.

Landers, Jane. *Atlantic Creoles in the Age of Revolutions*, Cambridge: Harvard University Press, 2011.

Landers, Jane. *Black Society in Spanish Florida*, Champaign, IL: University of Illinois Press, 1999.

Leffingwell, Dr. Albert and Charles Wesley Leffingwell. *The Leffingwell Record: A Genealogy of the Descendants of Lieut. Thomas Leffingwell, One of the Founders of Norwich, Conn.*, Aurora, NY: The Leffingwell Publishing Company, 1897.

Levin, Carole. *The Reign of Elizabeth I*. London: Palgrave, 2002.

Lillis, Bernard Joseph, "Forging New Communities: Indian Slavery and Servitude in Colonial New England, 1676 – 1776" (2012). Honors Theses - All. 903. http://wesscholar.wesleyan.edu/etd_hon_theses/903

Lynde, Benjamin. *The Diaries of Benjamin Lynde and of Benjamin Lynde, Jr.*, Cambridge: The Riverside Press, 1880.

Malcolm, Joyce Lee. *Peter's War: A New England Slave Boy and the American Revolution*, New Haven: Yale University Press, 2010.

Martin, John Frederick. *Profits in the Wilderness: Entrepreneurship and the Founding of New England*, Chapel Hill: University of North Carolina Press, 2014.

McGuire, Danielle L. *At the Dark End of the Street: Black Women, Rape, and Resistance, A New History of the Civil Rights Movement from Rosa Parks to the Rise of Black Power*, New York: Vintage, 2011.

Mead, Jeffrey. "Chains Unbound: Slave Emancipations in Greenwich Connecticut Online" (originally printed 1995), Chapter 1: Will Ye Even Sell Your Brethren? http://chainsunboundgreenwichct.blogspot.ca/2014/10/will-ye-even-sell-your-brethren-1995.html.

Newell, Margaret Ellen. *Brethren by Nature: New England Indians, Colonists, and the Origins of American Slavery*, Cornell University Press, 2015.

Noyes, Sybil, Charles T Libby, Walter G Davis. *Genealogical Dictionary of Maine and New Hampshire*, Baltimore: Genealogical Publishing Company, 2002.

Packard, Jerrold R. *American Nightmare: The History of Jim Crow*, New York: St. Martin's/Griffin, 2003.

Perkins, Mary E. *Old Houses of the Antient Town of Norwich, 1660-1800*, Norwich, CT: Press of the Bulletin Co., 1895

Perrault, Donald E. "Forgotten Voices: A History of Slavery in Saybrook, Connecticut". Masters Thesis, Wesleyan University, February 26, 1998.

Perry, Mark. *Lift Up Thy Voice: The Grimké Family's Journey from Slaveholders to Civil Rights Leaders*, New York: Penguin, 2003.

Petry, Elisabeth. *At Home Inside: A Daughter's Tribute to Ann Petry*, Jackson, MS: University Press of Mississippi, 2008.

Polakow, Amy. *Daisy Bates: Civil Rights Crusader*, New Haven: Linnet Books, 2003.

Prince, Bryan. *A Shadow on the Household: One Enslaved Family's Incredible Struggle for Freedom*, Toronto: McClelland & Stewart, 2009.

Redford, Dorothy Spruill. *Somerset Homecoming: Recovering a Lost Heritage*, Chapel Hill: University of North Carolina Press, 2000.

Rediker, Marcus. *The Slave Ship: A Human History*, New York: Penguin, 2008.

Reed, Annette Gordon. *The Hemingses of Monticello: An American Family*, New York: W.W. Norton, 2009.

Richardson, Douglas. *Plantagenet Ancestry: A Study In Colonial and Medieval Families*, Baltimore: Genealogical Publishing Company, 2011.

Rose, James. *Tapestry: A Listing History of the Black Family in Southeastern Connecticut*, Baltimore: Genealogical Publishing Company, 1977.

Salisbury, Edward Elbridge and Evelyn McCurdy Salisbury. *Family-Histories and Genealogies: A series of genealogical and biographical monographs on the families of MacCurdy, Mitchell, Lord, Lynde, Digby, Newdigate, Hoo, Willoughby, Griswold, Wolcott, Pitkin, Ogden, Johnson, Diodati, Lee and Marvin, and notes on the families of Buchanan, Parmelee, Boardman, Lay, Locke, Cole, De Wolf, Drake*, Bond and Swayne, Dunbar and Clarke, and a notice of Chief Justice Morrison Remick Waite, Vol. I, Part 2, New Haven: Tuttle, Morehouse & Taylor, 1892.

Salisbury, Edward Elbridge. *The Griswold Family of Connecticut*, New Haven: Tuttle, Morehouse & Taylor, 1884.

Schertz, Mary Fay Campbell. *The Lambrights: Descendants of Nicholas Lambright, a Revolutionary War Soldier*. Provo, UT: J. Grant Stevenson, 1977.

Schneider, Dorothy and Carl J. Schneider. *Slavery in America*, New York: Infobase Publishing, 2000.

Sigourney, Lydia. *Sketch of Connecticut, Forty Years Since*, Hartford: Oliver D. Cooke, 1824.

Simons, D. Brenton. *Witches, Rakes, and Rogues: True Stories of Scam, Scandal, Murder, and Mayhem in Boston, 1630-1775*, Beverly, MA: Commonwealth Editions, 2006.

Sparks, Randy J. *Africans in the Old South: Mapping Exceptional Lives across the Atlantic World*, Boston: Harvard University Press, 2016.

Speare, Elizabeth George. *The Witch of Blackbird Pond*, Boston: Riverside Press/Houghton Mifflin, 1958.

Stewart, James Brewer, Ed. *Venture Smith and the Business of Slavery and Freedom*, Amherst: University of Massachusetts Press, 2010.

Stuart, Andrea. *Sugar in the Blood: A Family's Story of Slavery and Empire*, New York: Penguin/Random House, 2013.

Talcott, Mary Kingsbury, editor. *The Talcott Papers*, Collections of the Connecticut Historical Society, Vol. 4, Hartford: 1892.

Thompson, Roger. *From Deference to Defiance: Charlestown, Massachusetts 1629-1692*, Boston: New England Historic Genealogical Society, 2011.

Walworth, Reuben Hyde. *Hyde Genealogy, or, The descendants, in the female as well as in the male lines, from William Hyde, of Norwich*, Albany: J. Munsell, 1864.

Waterbury, Jean Parker, ed. *The Oldest City: St. Augustine, Saga of Survival*, St. Augustine: St. Augustine Historical Society, 1983.

Weis, Frederick Lewis and Walter Lee Sheppard, Jr. *Ancestral Roots of Certain American Colonists Who Came to America Before 1700*, Baltimore: Genealogical Publishing Company, 2002.

Wharton, Edith. *Summer* (reprint; originally published 1917), Mineola, NY: Dover Publications, 2006.

White, Philip M. *American Indian Chronology: Chronologies of the American Mosaic*, Santa Barbara: Greenwod Publishing Group, 2006.

Wiencek, Henry. *An Imperfect God: George Washington, His Slaves, and the Creation of America*, New York: Farrar Straus Giroux, 2004.

Wiencek, Henry. *Master of the Mountain: Thomas Jefferson and His Slaves*, New York: Farrar Straus Giroux, 2013.

Wilkerson, Isabel. *The Warmth of Other Suns: The Epic Story of America's Great Migration*, New York: Vintage, 2011.

Wise, Steven M. *Though the Heavens May Fall: The Landmark Trial That Led to the End of Human Slavery*, New York: Da Capo Press, 2006.

Articles

Benson, Adam. "Descendants of Norwich slave, owner meet," *Norwich Bulletin*, March 2012, http://www.norwichbulletin.com/article/20120330/NEWS/303309901.

De Leon, Ferdinand. "When King was in town," *The Seattle Times*, January 16, 1994.

Campbell, Steve. "After 150 years, a dark chapter of Gainesville's past still stirs passions," *Star-Telegram*, October 7, 2012: https://web.archive.org/web/20121029032734/http://www.star-telegram.com/2012/10/07/4318523/after-150-years-a-dark-chapter.html.

d'Entremont, Clarence-J. "He Jumped Bail", *Yarmouth Vanguard* (April 11, 1989): http://www.museeacadien.ca/english/archives/articles/15.htm.

Web links

"Miner Descent: Capt. Matthew Beckwith": http://minerdescent.com/2010/05/14/matthew-beckwith/

"Tiger Talk with Rev. Samuel Berry McKinney", Greater Seattle Morehouse College Alumni Association: http://gsmcaa.org/tigertalk/20-questions-with-reverend-samuel-berry-mckinney-49/.

Biser, Margaret."What I learned from leading tours about slavery at a plantation" (June 29, 2015): http://www.vox.com/2015/6/29/8847385/what-i-learned-from-leading-tours-about-slavery-at-a-plantation.

D'Angelo, Daryl. "Polimom". "Mommy, Are We Black?" (October 2, 2005): http://www.polimom.com/2005/10/02/mommy-are-we-black/.

Downes, Torrance. "The Lyndes of London and Saybrook, via Boston": http://www.cypresscemeteryosct.org/lynde.html .

Ford, Dionne. "My family tree in black and white". *More* (2013): http://comingtothetable.org/wp-content/uploads/2013/10/My-Family-Tree_-In-Black-and-White-_-MORE-Magazine.pdf.

Hilden, Dr. Patricia Pen. "Hunting North American Indians in Barbados" (posted May 2002): http://realhistoryww.com/world_history/ancient/Misc/Barbados/

Hunting_North_American_Indians_in_Barba-
dos.htm.

Hinks, Dr. Peter. "Citizens All: African Americans in Connecticut 1700-1850", , http://cmi2.yale.edu/citizen-
s_all/stories/module1/documents/pdfs/mod-
_1_digging_deeper.pdf Holloway, Melinda. "Savagery in the Susquehanna, Frederick Stump" (2011):
https://talesinthetree.wordpress.com/2011/02/17/
savagery-in-the-susquehanna/ .

Mead, Jeffrey. "Hester Mead: An Uncommon Artist?", ,
1993 and 2009, http://meadburyingground-
s.blogspot.ca/2009/10/hester-bush-mead-uncom-
mon-artist.html.

Nielsen, Euell A. "BlackPast.org, Remembered & Reclaimed": *www.blackpast.org/?q=aah/haynes-lemuel-1753-
1833*.

Norton, Frederick Calvin. "Negro Slavery in
Connecticut" (originally published in *Connecticut Magazine*, Vol. 5, No. 6, June 1899): http://history.rays-
place.com/slavery.htm.

Pettee, Rev. David. "Ghosts of the Masters: Descendants of
Slaveholders Reckon with History" (May 14, 2011):
https://ghostsofthemasters.wordpress.com/
2011/05/14/a-case-study-in-researching-northern-
slaveholding-ancestry/.

St. Augustine Genealogical Society web site, Eusebius Fernando Bushnell baptism record: https://sagssupport-
.org/research/church-records/cathedral-
baptisms-1800-1899/.

The King Center, Atlanta, GA, "Speech to the Freedom
Riders", Sunday, May 21, 1961: http://www.theking-
center.org/archive/document/speech-freedom-rid-
ers#.

Media

Browne, Katrina. *Traces of the Trade: A Story from the Deep
North* (film documentary: June 24, 2008)

Resources

Coming to the Table: http://comingtothetable.org/

The Slave Dwelling Project: http://slavedwellingproject.org/

Gilder Lehrman Institute of American History: https://www.gilderlehrman.org/collection-search?field_keywords_-subjects=72822 .

National Museum of African American History and Culture: https://nmaahc.si.edu/ .

New England house museums which interpret former slave quarters and history for the public;

Bush-Holley House: http://www.greenwichhistory.org/bh_history

Hempstead Houses: https://www.ctlandmarks.org/hempsted
Royall House & Slave Quarters: http://www.royallhouse.org/

ALSO BY GRANT HAYTER-MENZIES

Woo, the Monkey Who Inspired Emily Carr: A Biography (Douglas & McIntyre, 2019)

Dorothy Brooke and the Fight to Save Cairo's Lost Horses (Potomac, 2017 and Allen & Unwin, 2018)

Mrs. Ziegfeld: The Public and Private Lives of Billie Burke (McFarland, 2016)

From Stray Dog to World War I Hero (University of Nebraska, 2015)

Lillian Carter: A Compassionate Life (McFarland, 2014)

Shadow Woman: The Extraordinary Career of Pauline Benton (McGill-Queen's University Press, 2013)

The Empress and Mrs. Conger: The Uncommon Friendship of Two Women and Two Worlds (University of Hong Kong, 2011)

Imperial Masquerade: The Legend of Princess Der Ling (University of Hong Kong, 2008)

ABOUT OLD JOHSON PLACE PUBLISHERS

We are writers who publish other writers. Our mission is to assist with projects by published writers who have a special project that their usual publishers find too long, too short, too strange, too uncommercial, or too difficult to classify. For those projects we select, we help our writers gain more control of the book than would be possible with a commercial publishers. Some projects are too important to be left to the priorities of profit.

www.ojppub.com

DISCARD